CW01315178

1001 Everyday Writing Prompts

That Will Help Motivate You Creatively

CHRISTINA ESCAMILLA

Copyright © 2020 by Christina Escamilla

All rights reserved. This book or any portion thereof may not be reproduced or used in any manner whatsoever without the author's express written permission.

All characters, names, places, and events in this book are fictitious unless otherwise noted. Any mention of real-world characters, names, businesses, and events has been made in an editorial facet. All information in this book is presented *as-is*. No representation or warranties surrounding further use of the information contained within this book has been drawn. Both the author and publisher shall not be liable for any endeavors taken up by these prompts in any degree whatsoever.

Table of Contents

Contents

Location, Location, Location. 3
- Home 4
- Famous Locales 11
- Unknown Regions 18
- Out of this World 26

Seasons, Holidays, & Special Occasions. 37
- Spring 37
- Summer 46
- Fall 58
- Winter 67
- Western Holidays 76
- Eastern Holidays 86
- Special Occasions 95

Nature in All its Forms 105
- The Weather 105
- Plants 114
- Waterways 121
- Geological Foundations 128
- Other Ecosystems 135

Emotions, Memory, and Things Unseen 142

Positive Emotions 143
Negative Emotions 151
The Future 160
The Past 167
Finding Inspiration 174
Characters of All Sorts 182
Personality Traits 182
Protagonists 191
Antagonists 198
Occupations 206
Sports, Animals, & Misc. 215
Playing Games 216
Sports of All Sorts 221
Wild Animals 226
Pets 231
Food 237
Finances 242
ABOUT THE AUTHOR 249

Location, Location, Location.

In fiction, location is everything. In many ways, the setting can even be considered a character in its own right. It helps to move the plot along, and it can work to define character attributes. Here are some prompts that all deal with the concept of location somehow, whether near or far.

Home

Many writers are of the mindset that their characters must leave home for anything good to happen. They believe that if their character has some kind of epic adventure, then the plot will automatically engage the reader; however, that doesn't always have to be the case. A developed story can happen in the comfort of one's home.

1. Your character is peacefully sleeping when the shrieking sound of their alarm awakes them. Hurriedly, they get out of bed and begin to get dressed, only to realize that they do not remember why they set the alarm in the first place. Wait...did they set it all?

2. Your character has friends and family coming over for a get-together, but the house is a mess! With just two hours to go until guests arrive, they have to decide where to start first, knowing that they cannot possibly get everything done in time. Will their friends and family judge them for the messy bits? Or will they have to hide it?

3. Your character finally settles in bed for some shut-eye. When they are about to fall asleep, loud music ruins their slumber. Try as they might, they cannot drown out the sound. It radiates around the house with loud and obnoxious beats. They can either try to find some inventive way to drown out the sound or confront their noisy neighbor.

4. After arriving home from a party, your character finds their entire house topsy turvy. The doors have become windows; the furniture is not only a different color but on the ceiling. The only thing that might seem familiar is your character's reaction.

5. Your character has been evicted! The current owner of the house is selling it and has not given them an advanced notice whatsoever. Your character can choose to start looking for a new place right away or fight eviction from the only home they've ever known.

6. In a similar scenario, suppose your character has opted to go house hunting. With so little time, envision a scenario in which they have a full set of houses lined up to view. While it sounds good in theory, only the worst of the worst fit into their budget.

7. While remodeling the inside of their home, your character finds a secret tunnel deep into the Earth. They work their way down to the very end, in which they find a strange secret, be it a treasure, the bones of a hapless victim, or something else entirely.

8. Your character excuses themselves at a friend's house to use the bathroom. Then it happens, their stomach cramps, and moments later, they've clogged up the toilet. Worse still, this night was strictly about making a good first impression.

9. Envision a scenario in which your character discovers what a 'home' or a shelter is, even if it's merely a cave sectioned on the side of a mountain; be it pre-historic or post-apocalyptic.

10. After an incredibly exhausting day at work, your character comes home to relax and unwind. Before they can do just that, they see themselves, another them, sitting on the couch – relaxing after a long day at work. Just what is going on here?

11. In a similar scenario, suppose your character comes home to find that their key does not work. After several attempts, they decide to just bang on the door out of frustration, even though they live alone. Surprisingly, someone does answer the door but insists that this is *their* home.

12. Your character is so bored that they decide to record a couple of vlogs (video blogs) of themselves, announcing their boredom to the world. They set up their camera equipment and begin recording; that's when things take an unexpected turn.

13. Your very hungry character is planning the perfect meal. Their perfect meal will consist of a medium-rare steak, lemon sautéed shrimp, basil pasta, a fresh kale salad, and all followed by a glass of red wine; perhaps a vegetarian or vegan dish if your character fancies it. They aren't celebrating anything special, but your character wants to treat themselves during their night-in. Dinner is almost ready; then, suddenly, the stove catches on fire.

14. Your character doesn't want to get out of bed. Every so often, they break into sobs and bury their face into the pillow. What has made them so upset?

15. The sound of loud meowing inside the house rouses a character from their slumber. They jump out of bed and immediately begin to investigate. They don't own a cat.

16. Imagine a similar scenario, but instead of one single cat, it's a menagerie of different animals (from lions to chipmunks, or whatever you prefer). What's curious is how they got there. Even more strange is the question of why they aren't eating each other.

17. Your character has a virus and spends all day coughing, sneezing, and hacking. However, there is one task inside their home that the character must accomplish. They strive towards completing this task despite their illness getting progressively worse. What is this task, and why are they so determined to finish it?

18. While rifling through items on their dresser, a character stumbles across something that makes them cry out in shock. Someone has hidden a video camera without their consent. Who might have committed this horrible deed, and what will your character do about it?

19. A couple of young characters are home alone when suddenly several explosions ring out in the distance. The kids immediately try to reach their parents, who are out shopping, but there is no answer. They cling to each other and look out the window. Unknowingly, they are about to witness the start of World War III.

20. Your character comes home to find roses leading to the bedroom upstairs. On the landing, they find a note and can't help but giggle to themselves. The writer promises the character an "interesting surprise." The character all but runs up the stairs, but on the bed is not the person they are expecting. The character has no idea who this person is.

21. A young couple is frantically rushing around the house, throwing clothes into bags while searching for the car keys at the same time. What has made them so troubled? Who or what are they escaping from?

22. Using the above scenario, suppose that the couple is in such a hurry because they have to rush to the hospital. The question is why; is it a baby, an illness, or a completely unforeseen circumstance?

23. Two roommates are notorious for pranking each other, filming it, and posting the videos online. Views come in from the millions. One of the roommates is conducting the best prank yet. It's too bad this prank is going to go so very wrong.

24. Your character watches their computer screen intently. The monitor displays several different feeds showing various people going about their daily lives. Unfortunately, none of these people know that they are being watched.

25. The year is 1938, and the *War of the World* radio broadcast has just aired over the radio. Many react in fear and mass hysteria. Take the perspective of one of these characters who has decided to hole up in their home and shoot anyone who chances by, assuming that all strangers are extraterrestrials from outer space.

26. Your character follows the sound of gurgling to their bathroom toilet. While they are dealing with that, a pipe in the kitchen bursts. Then, their showerhead pops off, and water begins rushing in. What else could go wrong?

27. Your character comes home after a long day of work. The only thing they want most is a quiet night in with the person they love. That plan is short-lived when they find their partner in bed with someone else.

28. After a long vacation, your character is shocked to discover their home has been burglarized. Since the initial break-in, a horde of spiders has also taken up residence all over the place.

29. Your character flips through movies, debating on what to watch. The subscription services they use have given them thousands of options, and still, they can't find anything suitable. That's when they see one piece that stands out, "The Life of You." Clicking on the title; they are shocked to see the opening scene is a birth. Wait a minute...it's their own.

30. Your character is struggling to make ends meet. Working three jobs only seems to pay the bare minimum. After work, they come home and throw the keys on the table, landing right next to a large bag of unmarked bills. How did the money get there? More importantly, what happens if they choose to keep it?

31. Your character finds themselves stuck in their own basement. No matter how hard they try, they can't seem to get out. How on earth did they find themselves in such a predicament? More importantly, what happens if no one hears their cries for help?

Famous Locales

Many places throughout the world are significant in some way. The following sites are famous because of the historic moment attached to them or the notable landmark they cover. No matter what, these places allow our characters to go beyond their quaint, sometimes mundane lives.

32. For years, your character has been training for this moment; they are scaling Mt. Everest. Many who have tried to have perished. Some of their bodies are still there. Will your character join this grim collection?

33. While on a tour of the Empire State building, your character sees a group of teenagers dropping something from over the edge of the private balcony. Upon inspection, the “something” is a collection of ballpoint pens. At this height, it could cause significant harm to anything and anyone below. What does your character do?

34. Your character is a spy, not just any spy, one of the very best. However, when the clock of Big Ben strikes 6 o’clock precisely, something even *they* can’t predict happens next.

35. Taking a deep breath and then clearing their throat, your character readies themselves. It’s now or never. The Eiffel tower makes a beautiful backdrop to their proposal. Working up the courage, they get down on one knee. However, before they can get a word out, a shot rings out.

36. Your character cradles their child close to their chest on a barely functioning boat. Up ahead is a beacon of hope, a chance to escape their war-torn country; the Statue of Liberty. Will they find a flourishing and enriching new life, or will they instead find themselves in a situation of hardship and turmoil?

37. The leaning tower of Pisa is one of the premier places to take a larger than life photo. Your character is attempting to "lean" against the building with the power of camera angles. The moment is short-lived when the tower falls behind them.

38. The Roman Colosseum is notorious for the gladiator games that once took place there. Perhaps they still do. Your character stumbles across a secret society that holds similar events in the middle of the night, using hapless victims as "gladiators."

39. A murder has just occurred at the Hollywood sign! Is it a celebrity? A tourist? No matter, your character is on the case!

40. Sadly, many suicides take place each year at the golden gate bridge. Your character has made a pact to save every life that they humanly can. After doing this religiously for 40 years, your character needs someone to save theirs.

41. Your character has given themselves an exciting and scary challenge to get themselves in better shape – to participate in the Great Wall Marathon in China! Being that it is one of the most challenging marathons globally, how will your character prepare themselves for the trip of a lifetime? What happens along the way and during the Great Wall Marathon?

42. For years, your character has been unable to see the person they love because of a strict government regime. However, all of that is about to change. The Berlin Wall is finally coming down!

43. One of the most famous but unexplained sites on Earth is Stonehenge. Although many popular theories exist regarding its origins and functions, it is still very mysterious. Craft a narrative in which your character is solely responsible for its design and execution.

44. The Taj Mahal was originally the mausoleum of Mumtaz Mahal, whom Shah Jahan had built for her. Suppose a young couple wanders through this place of "Undying Love" and comes across the spirit of this woman. She wants them to fulfill a favor, but what?

45. Your character is shooting a film in the middle of Times Square. Unbeknownst to them, they're about to film a terrorist attack.

46. Your character clutches the tiny hands of their child while running for their lives. Lava is closing behind them. The air is so thick and black, and it is almost suffocating. History will remember what happened to

Pompeii, but the character must only think of survival for now.

47. Your character has set up a tent at the grand canyon. Quite curiously, in the dead of night, someone has moved their position to the edge. Let's hope they are very, very careful upon waking.

48. Your character has gone to Las Vegas and loses it all. Including their means to get back home. Now, they find themselves sitting on a stoop crying, with the brilliant lights and signs as a backdrop. What are they going to do?

49. Your character excitedly whizzes in and out of each of the New Orleans shops. Annoyingly, they loudly declare to anyone that will listen that they don't believe in any of this "Voodoo nonsense." Other tourists and shopkeepers aren't the only ones who are listening. Spirits are too.

50. Pick a tragedy that has taken place in the city of your choosing. Now, write a story in which your character can change the course of history, or they can bear witness to this unfortunate moment.

51. In a small village just outside Mt. Fuji, your character has decided to take a quest. What is it they hope to accomplish, and why will this quest take them to the top of a mountain?

52. Mount Rushmore has four distinct Presidential heads carved on its surface. Make that 5. That is if a particular character gets their way. Yours.

53. What is the most famous location in your town? Craft a narrative that explores its features and surroundings so well that a nonlocal could easily spot the area based on your description alone.

54. Your character has been sent to prison for a crime they have not committed. After exhausting all legal aid and resources, they decided that their only option is to break out - of Alcatraz.

55. The Lascaux Cave in France holds some of the oldest paintings ever found. Craft a scenario in which your character is seeing them for the very first time. A day after they were created.

56. Suppose your character is a dancer at the infamous Moulin Rouge. The place is no stranger to strange drugs, extortion, and carnal sin, but everything is about to get much worse when a new stranger pays a visit.

57. It's considered the happiest place on Earth. Or is it? A tragedy is about to strike one of the world's most famous amusement parks, and no mouse ears in the whole place know what to do about it.

58. Your character is a famous actor who has finally gotten their star placed on the Hollywood Walk of Fame. This should be an honor, but the actor is deeply offended. They display their anger with a sledgehammer. What has got them so worked up?

59. There are thousands of museums across the world. Some are known for being unusual or downright creepy. Pick one of these places, the stranger the better, and envision a scenario in which your character gets trapped overnight.

60. Cemeteries might not be the most famous locales, nor the most lively (pun intended), but they make good story fodder. Use a well-known cemetery, research who might be buried there, and then craft a narrative about someone's life and unfortunate passing. Want to feel even more inspired? Visit this place. Remember to pick up any debris you see and bring fresh flowers for your selected person.

61. Your character has embarked on a year-long bucket list after being diagnosed with a terminal illness. Now they only have three more goals to accomplish.

These are the most dangerous items of all. Little does your character know; however, there has been an error with their test results. It turns out they are not dying from a disease after all. Will news reach them before it's too late?

Unknown Regions

Locations can sometimes be remote, obscure, and otherwise mysterious. The following prompts deal with places that exist outside normal society or have some strangeness that has happened there.

62. Your character is thirsty, so *very* thirsty. It's been days since they've had even a tiny drop. Help might come, but it sure would be hard in the middle of a desert.

63. A scuba diver is descending lower and lower into the murky, watery abyss. They are investigating a sunken ship, hoping to find gold. Instead, they find an array of pirate skeletons.

64. A character has been lost at sea for quite some time now. Finally, after what seems like an eternity, they spot land, and it doesn't take long before they are joyously running ashore, eager to see another living soul. Unfortunately, the last person on this island died centuries ago.

65. Your character has been backpacking across Asia when somehow they manage to veer off course. By a lot. Now, they are wandering through dense foliage. They have no idea where they are, location-wise, and the strange statues they have stumbled upon aren't helping to quell their anxiety.

66. It's cold. So very cold. Your character finds themselves huddled against their backpack in a frosty cave. How did they get there?

67. Your young character is on a family vacation. After leaving their beloved teddy bear behind, the character goes looking for their best pal. First sneaking out of the hotel room, and then wandering the streets of the city. Soon they are both scared and very, very lost—still no sign of Teddy.

68. In the middle of a wild and overgrown field, once home to a bounty of different crops, an old farmer can be found kneeling and crying. Besides the lack of produce, what has caused such great distress?

69. A couple is lying side by side on the bed of a pickup truck. Above them, stars twinkle in the night sky. It is utterly romantic. At least, for now. Something extraordinary is about to take place.

70. News reports are coming in all over town about a murderer on the loose. Suburban houses seem to be the target. A character who lives in such a dwelling decides to hole themselves in a shed out in the woods. It's remote enough. It just so happens to have also been built by the very criminal looking for shelter now.

71. Suppose the apocalypse has hit. A character has a remote bunker only about 20 miles away. There is enough food and water to last them for 40 years. Even some books and board games too. However, they must travel by foot. Will the character make it that far?

72. Two friends have a loud shouting match in the middle of the street. No one is quite sure what the argument is about, but it seems to be getting louder. Finally, one of the friends throws their hands up and furiously stalks off – right before falling into an open utility hole.

73. Your character has joined the search for a missing child. It's a harrowing and upsetting experience, of course. It also quickly turns very confusing. The child is found in one of the darkest parts of the woods. Although the child returns home safely, something seems a little *off*. Your character is the only one who seems to notice.

74. Your character holds the hand of a dying loved one. They and their loved one have chosen to live 100 miles from the nearest town, which means 100 miles away from the nearest hospital. The decision will cost them dearly.

75. Your character conducts face-to-face, at-home interviews for their company. They come across one street that seems further than the last time they remember it. As they walk up, the road appears to get further and further away. With each step, the houses just...slide into the distance. Just what in the world is going on?

76. At the edge of town, there is a shop that doesn't seem to have any customers. Even more curiously, there is no website address, no phone number listed, and the simple signage does not indicate what niche this store might fulfill. Finally, your character walks into the shop, eager to find answers. That is when they are transported *elsewhere.*

77. Your character has been a city dweller their entire life. However, they take a job at a rural, remote location. Craft a narrative in which they try and cope with this new reality.

78. It's freezing. Your character is practically ice, and the temperature continues to drop. What is most strange about their predicament is that they live in a tropical environment that never climbs above 70 degrees Fahrenheit.

79. Envision a scenario in which your character is a knight just thrown from their horse. Not only do they hit the ground hard, but their once-trusty steed has now run off. Your character is left to wander in a wild and untamed wilderness.

80. In a similar scenario, suppose your character is a cowboy who has done a few misdeeds. Now the law is also hot on their tail. How do they escape with no horse?

81. Your character discovers a vehicle floating in the middle of a lake while out jogging. Their first reaction, of course, is to call the police, but then they realize that someone is calling out for help. Do they venture into the unknown depths themselves, or do they go ahead with their plan to call for help?

82. In this scenario, take the perspective of an abducted child. They have managed to escape but are lost in the wilderness. From a close-person perspective, envision a scenario in which they must struggle to survive, and ultimately do.

83. Your character is a marine biologist that has been given a chance of a lifetime – study the deepest part of the ocean, the Mariana trench, exclusively. However, during the first few minutes of descending, something goes wrong, and if they do not gain control of the vessel, their research and their life will be lost.

84. Police sirens blare, and gunshots ring out. It is a prison escape! In this scenario, take the criminal's perspective or the agent sent to track them down. In an exciting twist, you can even switch between the perspective of the two.

85. Your character has been boasting about their survival skills for quite some time. Now that they are on a rather unexpected camping trip that goes awry, other hungry campers beg the character to help them find food. If the character refuses, they might all starve. The problem is – the character doesn't know the first thing about survival.

86. Let's reverse the above prompt. Suppose the character *does* know a great deal about survival, only they are left alone after the other campers unwittingly eat poisonous berries. How does the character cope with such a loss?

87. Yo ho ho, a pirate's life…isn't all that it's cracked up to be. Your character is a shipmate that has just endured an all-out assault from another ship. Thankfully, they manage to survive. Barely. Unfortunately, they are the only one who does.

88. Your character wants to explore one of the few unmapped caves in the world. They put together a team of close friends and accomplished adventurers and embark on what will be a grueling yet enriching journey. It's a decision they will soon regret as a collapse occurs and they find themselves trapped below the Earth's surface.

89. Your character wakes up in a strange room that they don't remember going to bed in. What's worse is that they cannot seem to escape the room. With anxiety setting in, they are desperate to get out by any means possible. How do they do so, and more importantly, how did they get there in the first place?

90. Suppose your character finds themselves wandering a town that they have never been in before. Before long, they come across a telephone pole with a missing poster attached. The person's picture is their own.

91. While traveling, your character comes across a remote village. So distant that they can't seem to locate it on any map. If that wasn't strange enough, these townspeople believe your character is a deity of some sort. No matter what your character says, the people here are keen on offering a sacrifice.

92. In a similar scenario, consider one of the many civilizations that have been untouched by the modern world. As of this writing, there are a little under 100, including the most famous Sentinelese. Your character has unwittingly stumbled across a remote tribe, and most now communicate that they have no ill intentions but merely want to find their way back home.

93. When birds begin showing up on an unnamed character's lawn, their first instinct is to call animal control. Then they notice that each bird has something valuable in its beak. One has a money clip, another an expensive-looking necklace, and so on. Against their own better judgment, the character begins to follow the birds. Where do these feathered friends take them?

94. Over the river and through the woods...wait, this isn't right. Your character is sure that their grandmother is supposed to live in *this* area. However, they can't seem to locate the small cottage. The more they look, the more lost they get. Will your character ever get to grandma's house?

Out of this World

Sometimes we need our characters to leave their homes to have exciting moments happen. Did I say home? I mean planet. Or perhaps in another reality or world altogether. These prompts all occur in a world beyond our own. This might be on a space station, a land merely unheard of, a fantastic region, or roaming somewhere in a nearby galaxy. Sometimes these prompts may also contain strangeness or magic that make reality bend.

95. A group of cosmonauts has created a robot to help them on their mission to Mars. However, unbeknownst to these explorers, the robot has been reprogrammed before take-off, and upon arrival, it will seek to sabotage the mission.

96. A young character has to play outside after getting into trouble inside. They are quite reluctant to do so until they come across a small, abandoned spacecraft. Where do they go, and what do they find there?

97. An astronaut crash lands on a plant that looks exactly like Earth. That is, except for one small but significant detail. What is it, and how long does the astronaut take them to notice?

98. After contacting an alien species, your character becomes an ambassador on behalf of Earth. It is a tough job, considering how unique and diverse the human species is. The position is even more challenging, considering the alien race does not want peace.

99. The trope, *cowboys in space,* is popular amongst science fiction fans. In this scenario, craft your unique take on gunslingers in the stars by adding another classic trope to it. If you are unsure what a trope is, it is an overused and common plot device. Make it unique and well written to break the mold of mundanity. For instance, you can add the hero's journey to the mix by making one of these cowboys responsible for a stowaway who does not want to be helped.

100. Your character unwittingly finds themselves transported to another planet. Not only do they have to work out how this came to be, but now your character must explain to the native planet populace that they mean no harm.

101. Trips to outer space are one day going to be as common as traveling from one country to another, give or take 50 years for this prediction to come true. Envision a scenario in which your character is about to experience commercial space travel for the first time.

102. An astronaut is the last member of their crew left alive after an explosion occurs. Oxygen is dwindling, and all hope seems lost. In this scenario, take the astronaut's perspective and pen a final goodbye to the person they love the most. Make sure you also include what exactly went wrong.

103. In a similar scenario, suppose that, although there is no way to save the rest of the crew, the astronaut finds some way to protect themselves. How do they go about it?

104. Your character is on the first expedition to Mars. Along the way, the navigational controls fail, and the crew lands on an entirely different planet or moon.

105. Your character is a scavenger in a space colony on the moon. The Earth now uses the moon to store trash, and it has become a junkyard. While scavenging, your character stumbles across something that both amazes and terrifies them.

106. Your character is a scientist researching black holes. One of their goals is to be able to create, maintain, and control such a phenomenon. One day, they make a breakthrough and manage to create an ant-sized black hole. A second later, everything in the container is sucked up through the pinhole. Then the lab that was containing the chamber. Then the building the lab was in. What happens next? Will the entire Earth soon be destroyed?

107. Your character is a noble from Neptune. They are tasked with creating peace negotiations with Mercury, their enemy planet. Going over there would be suicide, but not going could spell doom as Mercury is known for their mass heat bombs, powerful enough to wipe out all of Neptune's population. What will your character do?

108. Your character and their space crew land on Europa, one of Jupiter's moons. They are studying the area for any sign of life in the ocean underneath the ice. While researching, they hear a strange melody. Soon, their crewmate is hypnotized, and are compelled to go into the Europan ocean. Soon, your character follows suit, unable to resist the alien siren's call.

109. For centuries, your character has done the same thing over and over again; they eat planets. Yes, they *eat* planets. After eating a blue and green world with lots of little creatures on it, your character moves on to the one with rings. This time a loud booming voice stops them, and the character soon finds themselves in a glass dome. A massive eye looks at them and demands punishment. For this piece of weird fiction, try to concentrate on a location that would allow a giant character to eat planets and an even bigger character. Perhaps a deity, maybe large aliens.

110. On Planet Gaze, everyone has six eyes, 4 in the front and 2 in the back. While climbing a mountain for leisure, your character loses their footing and falls. The accident leaves them with only two eyes. How significantly does life change for them?

111. Your character and their friends are swimming through the galaxy. They stop playing when they see a metal monster feeding on helpless human explorers through its wired tentacles. Will your character and their group of friends save these fellow astronauts or escape before it's too late?

112. Outside of one of the space station windows, an astronaut sees a nearby planet suddenly appear in their line of sight. Stranger still, the giant orb disappears and reappears somewhere else. It happens again and again. The astronaut decides to visit the planet to investigate this strange phenomenon up close.

113. An astronaut crash-lands into what could be considered the universe's salvage yard. Ships, large pieces of metal, and other strange objects are all dumped here. Your character must find various tools amongst the wreckage to find a way home.

114. In this scenario, Artificial Intelligence has finally reached the point where you cannot tell robots from humans. Take the perspective of one of these cybernetic beings and consider how strange life might be if you are just experiencing it for the first time.

115. Envision a scenario in which several worlds are not only on good terms with one another but conduct intergalactic trade. Your character is carrying imports into one such world, but there is a problem. The planet doesn't seem to have the right currency, and it is dire that your character receives precisely the right amount. Otherwise, their boss will be very, *very* unhappy.

116. Your character is an astronaut uninterested in exploring intelligent worlds for their culture or studying the language. No, they cannot be bothered with any part of further exploration. Instead, they have a mission to find all the cool bars.

117. Strangely, your character suddenly finds themselves hurtling towards Earth. No, they are not an astronaut engaging in the world's highest freefall. If not, then who are they, and why are they falling?

118. Your character has agreed to be one of the first people to inhabit Mars for a scientific study. However, while on the way, the spaceship veers off course, and your character and the rest of the crew suddenly find themselves inhabiting a planet no one even knew existed.

119. Your character is a young teen that grew up listening to stories of an ancient beast that lives just outside the village. Beyond the creature are supposedly rich gardens full of delicious fruits and vegetables. When a famine hits, your character decides they will best the monster.

120. After years of living in the same house, your character finally decides to travel the world. However, rather than merely going to new cities or countries, they are about to embark on a journey through the unseen world, where magic is real.

121. Your character seeks the help of an alchemist, desiring a potion that will help them find love. However, when they drink the first potion, they are suddenly transported to a strange world. When they take another gulp, they are back in the alchemist's shop. The alchemist apologizes and gives them something else to drink. The same thing happens. As it turns out, this alchemist is the alchemist's assistant.

122. There are two types of beings in this world, those that live in the water and those that live on land. Your character is somehow caught in the middle and must find a way to make peace between both fractions.

123. Your character has inherited a garden from an estranged family member. Although they have heard of their family member's prized nursery, they have never actually seen it. When they finally do, it's like nothing they've ever seen before in their life. Even the plants seem to be out-of-this-world. Perhaps they are.

124. A rookie cop is dodging a hail of bullets from a gang of bank robbers. Unfortunately, they are shot and instantly lose all consciousness. Rather than waking up in a regular hospital, they wake up in a woodland infirmary, cared for by strange fairies.

125. Your character is on a long trek to save a princess. In this scenario, suppose that they must go through three different fantasy worlds to complete their quest. Make each more dangerous and treacherous than the last.

126. Down on their luck, your character decides to commit burglary for the first time. Their neighbors are rich and noticeably absent most of the time, so why not? Your character gets more than they bargained for when they sneak through the window of their neighbor's house and suddenly find themselves in a strange fantasy land.

127. Your character is running a marathon, which is something they do almost every season. However, this time it seems like things aren't going as planned. Even though they studied the race map extensively and there are signs everywhere, they still get lost. Soon they find themselves in a strange place, and the more they try to find their way out, the more lost they become.

128. Your character is a botanist sent to study strange mushrooms that have been growing throughout the European countryside. Moving them could potentially hurt the plants, so your character decides to analyze them on-site. This doesn't seem to be problematic at first. Then the gnomes start coming out—lots and lots of gnomes.

129. Everything's coming up roses, and at night, lilies. Your character lives in a world made of plants, including themselves. While sunbathing for food, the dew from their pitcher plant TV shows images of a rock covered mass hurtling towards this extra-green planet. Soon everything goes black. How will your plant-species character survive?

130. Being a deep-sea mermaid can be pretty isolating. Your character is one such creature and has heard rumors from squids and whales about strange beings that lack fins and flippers. They decide to traverse to the top. At first, the character doesn’t see anything, but they feel vibrations before a loud shriek rings out, causing the waves to slosh around. They aren’t aware that it is a boat carrying these strange beings.

131. All fairies in the forest fly. Almost anyway. One fairy is terrified of heights and must find another way to go up and down the trees to earn their keep. How do they do so?

Seasons, Holidays, & Special Occasions.

If there is one thing that unites all cultures, it is an innate love for getting together and making merriment. There seem to be three universal aspects of holidays: food, fellowship, and decorations. These vary from culture to culture, of course, but they seem to be the most significant commonality. We also let the seasons dictate what we will celebrate and why. Prompts in this section will deal with certain aspects of the four seasons and the unique holidays and special occasions we love.

Spring

Ah, new life is in the air – whether little bundles of joy from the animal kingdom to wildflowers growing unfettered. Spring is a special time of rejuvenation and newness, which these prompts all work to embrace.

132. Your character is enjoying a pleasant bike ride across the park. That is until they hit something and fly headfirst over their handlebars. What, or who is it that they have hit? More importantly, are they okay?

133. There is an array of excellent products at the farmer's market to choose from, all at affordable prices. Plus, your character will be helping the local community. However, every time your character bites into a fruit or vegetable, it instantly becomes rotten.

134. Imagine that your character is selling at a farmer's market and is known for their large, oversized produce. However, your character soon finds out that their customers aren't buying your offerings to eat, but not because they are bad. What is the cause, and how does your character react?

135. Your character dons their favorite sunhat and visits a nearby famous garden. It's notable because of the large, man-eating plants and the poisonous flowers that are everywhere. So, your character had better be careful!

136. Every day, your character fills up the bird feeder for their little feathered visitors. Birds of all varieties come far and wide for the abundance of nuts, seeds, and fruits. However, today your character notices that no birds come by—the same thing with the next day and the next. Soon, your character goes on a mission to investigate.

137. "Let's go fly a kite, up to the highest hei-" Oh dear! That's much too high! Your character is a small child who is now being dragged by a massive dragon kite, proving that big is not always best.

138. It's the annual kite flying competition! Your character has won 2 of the last four matches they have entered. Their main competitor has also won two, thus, making this year the ultimate tiebreaker. Will your character win, and if so, what grand prize will they receive?

139. Your character is the star player of a local little league baseball team. Just before the big game, they break their arm, and as the pitcher, this will ultimately cause the team to have a disadvantage. How does your young character cope? If they cannot play, how else do they support their team?

140. Your character is a worn-down coach who was once one of the best in their sport. They used to lead their team to victory, but they seem to have lost all the zest they had for the game in the last decade or so. This year they will be retiring. Can they muster up the strength for one last win?

141. Spring is certainly in the air! Your character knows this because all of their friends seem to be coupling up. Even the animals are running off to bring in new life. This has been making your character feel incredibly lonely. They decide to be brave and try an unusual way to get a date. What is it?

142. Your character is engaging in a little spring cleaning. First, they do surface level touch-ups, scrubbing the counters, vacuuming, washing the dishes, etc. Then they tackle the rest of the house. Strangely enough, the more they clean, the more the house seems to grow dirtier. It seems their home is now twice as messy by the end of the day.

143. While spring cleaning, your character finds several boxes that they do not remember ever storing. These could have come from another family member, but it doesn't seem likely. What's even more unusual is the fact that the boxes all contain strange, never-before-seen artifacts.

144. Your character is shopping at a flea market and stumble across an old lamp. It works and has an interesting pattern on the shade, so they decide to take it home. However, when they turn the light on, it emits a strange blue hue that changes to red with the character's mood. Weird.

145. Suppose your character has a small clothing boutique and is having a big spring sale. They want to make room for new summer looks that should be arriving any day now. However, they get a customer demanding winter clothes; thick woolly sweaters and faux fur coats. Strangely, the customer isn't taking a vacation to a colder place, nor are they moving to a colder climate. So, why do they need such warm clothes?

146. Spring is often a time for new beginnings. To make further changes in one's life, whether physical cleaning, cutting out toxic people, entering into a new relationship, and so on. Suppose your character will make a drastic change in their life, whether or not it affects the people around them. What is their growth, and how do others react?

147. During a spring storm, your character decides to play in the rain. All is going well until the rain picks up until it's a full-blown monsoon. Now, your character can't see a foot in front of them and are becoming more lost.

148. In a similar scenario, suppose your character is one amongst a group of children playing in the rain. Thankfully, it doesn't storm, but the weather does cause another misfortune to occur. What exactly happens?

149. Your character has decided to get a new furry friend and visits their local pet store. Thinking they might walk away with a new kitten or puppy, they shock everyone they know when they come back with a new species entirely.

150. While walking home in a crowded city, your character stumbles across a little box that reads "Free 2 Good Home." Inside are three little puppies. In a moment of altruism, your character takes the animals home. The next day, there is a new box—this time with four kittens. Again, your character takes them home. On the third day, there is a box with five guinea pigs.

151. A maternity ward seems overwhelmed when a rash of babies are born. What is most strange is that no one has come for a pregnancy. The babies have just *appeared*. Just what is going on?

152. Your character is out collecting wildflowers when they accidentally run into a bee's nest. Not only are they severely allergic, but they can't seem to hide anywhere. The bees are soon closing in.

153. Your character is a beekeeper that is doing their part to protect this vital species. Not only are their conservation efforts admirable, but they also have an endless supply of delicious honey. That is, until one morning when they awake to find all but one of their hives missing.

154. Your character has decided to pop the question in a field of wildflowers since their beloved is a plant enthusiast. Unwittingly, however, your character is unaware that all of these flowers are poisonous.

155. While at a butterfly exhibit, your character suddenly hears the sound of children shrieking. Then adults follow suit. Something is wrong with the butterflies! While they are usually docile and gentle creatures, it seems as though the tables have turned! It looks like they no longer have a taste for nectar, but something else...*blood!*

156. Allergies have hit your character hard. They now live in a word of sneezing, coughing, and runny, irritable eyes. That is why they are so eager to try a new medication when it becomes available. It's too bad the side-effects include changes to their personality. Soon no one can recognize them anymore.

157. Your character is on a picnic when ants attack! First, these little creatures carry off a few carrot sticks, then some sandwiches, and even a whole watermelon. It would seem cartoony if it weren't so disturbing. Then one of the children gets carried away by the thousands of little insects.

158. Your character is throwing a large spring picnic for their neighborhood. They have spent weeks planning the shindig, including ordering custom decorations and an array of food. On the day of, they wait expectantly, a perfectly crafted lemonade in hand, but after a few hours, it's apparent that no one is coming.

159. Your character is out on the trail, eager to get some hiking in now that the weather is warming. They hear a grumble before nearby foliage starts crunching. It seems a bear has awakened from hibernation.

160. Spring is the perfect time for photographers to take pictures! Nature stands with a brilliant array of colors, like a painter's best canvass. However, when your character finally loads their photos, they see something they didn't catch before. Something most foul.

161. While working in their garden, your character comes across a note from almost a century ago. It can be a love letter, a business note, or anything else you can think of. Hoping the recipient might still be alive, your character goes on a quest to deliver it personally.

162. Your character is exploring a large abandoned estate when they come across a hidden garden. Your character finds a humanoid effigy made out of flowers among the ruins of marble benches and statues. When your character approaches it, the figure turns its head.

163. Once every season, your character has a big spring bounty to celebrate the passing of winter. During this particular feast, a bombshell drops. What is the news, and is it good or bad?

164. A dispute between neighbors occurs regarding the property line. Each homeowner believes that the other is responsible for cutting a small section of overgrown flowers. Finally, your character has had enough and mows down all of the flowers in the middle of the night. Not only do they bag them up, but they also flower-bomb the entirety of their neighbor's lawn. This isn’t going to end well.

165. On a beautiful spring evening, your character stands outside of the window of their love, belting out a beautiful sonnet that they wrote themselves. In it, they ask for the hand of the one they hold most dear. Not only do they have the wrong house, but the occupant eagerly accepts.

166. After a rainstorm, your character is collecting worms into a bucket. It's a slippery, slimy, disgusting mess, but your character is young, and this is how they have chosen to pass the time. It may pay off because they also discover a gold bar.

167. To raise money, a group of teens is having a carwash. All is going well, and they are making a decent amount of money, but soon things take a strange and unexpected turn. A car rolls up, and the driver acts suspiciously, maybe because their windshield has blood all over it.

168. Your character is perusing items at a garage sale, surprised to find such amazing deals on things that seem fresh out of the box. When sirens blare behind them, the owner of the house takes off running, tripping over the for-sale sign your character didn't seem to notice at first. Your character is about to witness the takedown of a criminal; who has been selling stolen goods at various houses listed on the real estate market.

169. Your character is spending a relaxing day at the lake, feeding the ducks and enjoying the warm weather. The day would have ended peacefully if your character hadn't noticed the body in the water.

Summer

This is the season of action, whether taking a family vacation or deciding now is the time for a new business venture. These prompts all deal with summer's action-oriented nature, from taking adventurous hikes to taking a swim at the lake.

170. Your character is kayaking down a river when the speed begins to pick up. What was otherwise a peaceful drift turns into a cataclysm of sharp turns and huge waves. Your character completely forgot about the marker they were supposed to be looking out for.

171. The tent is all set up, the s'mores making materials are ready, but there is just one problem – no one thought to pack any toiletries.

172. Your character is sleeping peacefully inside their tent when they wake to the sound of a moving brush. At first, they assume it might be a raccoon, skunk, or some other nocturnal animal. However, the noise gets louder; the leaves crunching hard underneath heavy footfalls. Timidly, they peak out of their tent, expecting to see a wolf. It isn't. It's the infamous Bigfoot.

173. At a summer retreat, your character comes across the activity they have been dreading for an entire week – the obstacle course. They look on the climbing wall, tire hop, and mud run with sheer terror. At the same time, conquering this fear would be tremendous.

174. Your character has been out exploring around the campsite and now can't find their way back. Does moss grow on the north or south side? Should they follow the birds? Find a river? Shrieking, they begin to run blindly down a direction chosen at random.

175. Your character is out for summer break! Excitement *should* ensue, but they soon find themselves very, very bored at home. This causes them to do something incredibly drastic. What activity do they engage in, and how do their parents/guardians react when they arrive home?

176. In a similar vein, suppose that your character is on vacation with their family in a crowded city far from home. Somehow your character manages to get separated from the group. To make matters worse, they don't speak the local language.

177. Your character has decided to take a staycation instead of their usual trip. They figure that a bit of relaxation should do them a world of good. At least, that was the idea. It seems everyone from the mailman to their neighbor wants to pester them for something.

178. A violent thunderstorm rocks the sea while your character is on a cruise ship. Even the captain didn't predict this turbulent system moving in. When everyone is encouraged to get below deck, your character finds themselves thrown overboard.

179. Using the theme of a cruise ship again, suppose your character finds a secret room that only staff should use. There they find some horror that others on board don't know about. What is this terrible secret that they have found out? Will they make it to shore before staff finds out they know?

180. Your character is trying their hand at surfing for the very first time. They pick it up well enough, but they accidentally hit something big and bulky underneath the water on one of their wipeouts. It's a shark.

181. Your character's vacation takes them somewhere very cold, with lots of snow and ice. While exploring one of the snowy water banks, your character spots an iceberg that looks like a chair made of glass. Asking their friend to take a picture of them, they quickly hop on, not realizing they've dislodged it by happenstance. Now they are drifting out to sea.

182. Your character wants a summer beach tan but doesn't want to sit under the hot sun for it. Instead, they hit up their local salon. After settling in on the tanning bed, they start to feel hot. *Really* hot.

183. Your character is *pissed.* They had the perfect summer planned, and their dream "summer glow" was the first on the list. However, after using a ton of sunscreen, your character ends up with blisters and a patchy sunburn. How did this happen?

184. "Could you take those stupid things off when I'm talking to you?" Your character is staring at their reflection, angry and distorted in someone else's sunglasses. What is your character mad about, and how will the other person respond?

185. Your character was resting by the bonfire at a summer camping retreat. They are happily lounging when they jerk with a start, hearing a rustling in the bushes. Not only are they the only ones awake, but out of the darkness comes something that makes them scream.

186. The heatwave has been going for almost a full month now, and it's not even July yet. Even through the long nights, the heat only intensified. With each report that comes out, the temperature is climbing. Will it ever end?

187. While taking your character is taking their brand new car out for a summer cruise, someone sharply almost hits them, causing your character to serve right into a fire hydrant. As water spurts out everywhere, they realize that the broken fire hydrant and crashed car isn't the only thing to worry about. What else has them spooked?

188. One early summer morning, your character realizes that their air conditioning has stopped working. Your character immediately checks on the children, but soon they realize that the children have managed to take matters into their own hands – finding a quite unusual way to stay cool.

189. Speaking of broken air conditioners, suppose your character decides to call a repair person only to open the door and see their ex. Is this going to be super awkward, or will sparks begin to fly again?

190. Your character begins to feel queasy and sits down on a nearby bench at the amusement park. Was it all the sugar drinks? The rides? Or, all the saltwater they accidentally swallowed on River Raft Adventurer? Whatever the case, they don't look so good.

191. Your character went sailing for the first time in what felt like forever. Suddenly, something big and reflective gleamed from under the waves. Before your character could make out what was below the water, they crash right into it.

192. A group of teens is hooting with delight as they light smoke bombs, ground spinners, and other fireworks. It's not even close to the 4th of July, let alone past 6 pm, and the madness has already begun. Your character walks in the opposite direction, but then a scream rings out.

193. The fireworks explode across the night sky. It's beautiful. Stunning. Your character is feeling super romantic and whispers, "I love you." To which the other character responds with, "I want to break up." Ouch!

194. In an attempt to be neighborly, your character visits a child's lemonade stand. It's a hot summer day, so the promise of a 50 cent cold drink sounds perfect anyway. However, when a character reaches into their pocket and looks back, they see a gun pointed up at them. A six-year-old is robbing them!

195. Your character is having a relaxing day at the pool when someone begins to scream. More screams ring out. There's something in the water, and it isn't like any animal your character has ever seen in their life.

196. "They always loved the beach," your character says solemnly, giving a eulogy. The funeral service for their elder relative is sad, but there is no denying the gorgeous scenery. That is until the deceased comes back to life.

197. Your character clasps the hand of their beloved and meanders along the boardwalk, night setting in over the ocean. Suddenly they hear a thud right next to them. Their partner has had a heart attack. This is tragic, but perhaps your character can save their lover.

198. The air is whistling through their hair and your character's squeals of delight ring out across the river. This is their first time tubing, and if they aren't careful, this may very well be their last. Up ahead are hazardous rocks.

199. Your character planned an exciting summer vacation for their family, even going as far as renting a beautiful lake house; however, after receiving the keys and opening up the place, the entire family screams. Not only is the whole area ransacked, but in the middle of the living room, a ravenous bear is still searching for food.

200. After failing most of their classes, your character has decided to do a 180 and tries to be a good student.

This task will prove difficult because the same kids they have been wasting time with are also in summer school.

201. While out for a leisurely walk, your character sees a classmate skipping rocks alone at the lake. This classmate is a real, strange egg. No one dislikes them, but they don't seem to have any friends either. Your character takes a deep breath and decides it's time to change that. They walk over and extend their hand in greeting.

202. What started as a fun evening of sharing ghost stories over the campfire suddenly ends with your character's weak-hearted best friend ending up in an ambulance.

203. "Go, go go!" Your character shouts, egging their friend on as they shove another s'more into their mouth. The s'more eating competition had been going well until one of the campers begins to choke violently.

204. On the subject of s'mores again, suppose your character is eating one for the very first time. It was at that moment that your character realizes that they are allergic to marshmallows.

205. Your character has finally made it onto the bass fishing circuit and is now fishing with the greats. However, on the day of the competition, everything goes wrong. First, the line breaks, then a hook ends up someone's nether regions, and finally, someone falls off the boat.

206. With greasy, sauce-stained fingers, your character is digging into ribs at the best barbecue joint in town. They can't stop scarfing down food! It's almost as if the sauce itself is addictive. That's because it is.

207. After a horrible car crash, your character finds themselves lost and hungry in a deep forest. It has been three days, and help doesn't seem to be on the horizon. They need to make a game plan for food, but they have a portable grill and the entire woods.

208. Your character is appalled when they go to the beach and see a large group taunting an overweight person in a bikini. Your character knows that downright yelling at them isn't going to prove a point. What do they do instead?

209. Suppose your character is the one teased. This time they decide to get their revenge in the most exciting way possible. They become a model, and when they become famous, they go back to the same beach, looking for those people.

210. Your character is a teen who has never kissed. All of that is just about to change. Fireworks are bursting overhead, they have their favorite cold drink in hand, and now their crush is leaning in close. Your character closes their eyes, puckers up, but then the unexpected happens. They suddenly get very ill, right on their crush.

211. The sky is grey and lifeless. Your character, a ship captain, is already watching the heavens for unexpected bad weather. That is when dozens and dozens of packages fall from the sky. What do they hold?

212. There are displays of rocks, insects, and even a few animal skulls at the nature center. Even better, there are dozens of trails that lead to possible animal habitats. If one is lucky, they might see a rabbit, fox, or deer. Perhaps if one is unlucky, they might also see the mysterious creature that lurks in the forest.

213. "You keep on smilin', sunshine." It was the last words your character heard before their beloved disappears at sea. Now that they are an adult, they are determined to set sail and determine what happened and why.

214. Summer is supposed to be a time for fun in the sun. Not this year. Since the end of May, it has been snowing nonstop. This is weird, not to mention downright scary, especially because you live so close to the equator.

215. Your character is sitting alone on the sand, letting the waves tickle their feet. Suddenly, two shells wash up on the coastline beside them: one broken and dull, the other shiny and pristine. Your character decides to pick one up, not realizing that, based on the choice, something incredible is about to happen.

216. By the time your character makes it to the beach resort, the evening has already set in. They begin simultaneously unpacking and making plans for their first vacation activities. The Television show they are watching cuts out with the "breaking news report." Your character gulps before looking around and hoping they are not alone. They aren't.

217. Even though your character is an adult, they have never learned how to swim. All of that is about to change! They have signed up for swimming classes at the local community pool. It's too bad they didn't realize that they signed up for the wrong age group, not realizing their error until they are standing side-by-side with toddlers.

218. Your character shyly takes off the last bit of clothing. They are going skinny dipping for the first time; their friends have convinced them. Your character doesn't think it's so bad until something in the water grabs them and pulls them under.

219. Your character is parasailing over the shiny ocean waves. They feel free as a bird until a whole flock of them begin attacking your character for no reason. If these birds continue, your character will plummet 25 feet.

Fall

This happens to be my absolute favorite season. There's something magical about the leaves changing colors, the night crawling in faster, and the cold drifting in. These prompts touch on the ethereal nature of Fall.

220. Your character is walking through a pumpkin patch, holding their lovers' hand, when the glint of moonlight reflects on the face of an already lit pumpkin. The odd decoration opens its mouth and speaks.

221. While driving down a lonely road, your character's tire blows out unexpectedly, and they crash into a nearby ravine. From somewhere above them, they hear the sound of scuffling feet. "They'll make a fine feast." A voice whispers in the darkness.

222. Your character and their grandma are knitting quietly by the fire. It isn't long before she falls asleep and begins to snore peacefully. Your character doesn't want to wake her and begins to pack up all the knitting equipment, but that is when their grandmother opens her mouth and whispers a dark ancient secret.

223. Your character sits around the dinner table, the cornucopia filled with fruits and nuts of all shapes and sizes. Soon the feast will begin. What the other guests do not know is that there is also a note inside.

224. Your character is carving pumpkins with a group of friends, trying to get ready for an upcoming party. They pull out one pumpkin at a time before stumbling across a once carved pumpkin; strangely, someone has taken the time to stitch it back together.

225. The leaves have turned brilliant shades of brown, yellow, and orange, and they crunch underneath your character's feet when they walk. Typically, they enjoy the sound, but not when they are trying to escape from someone.

226. Through the sound of rain, your character gets a phone call. Someone they love is now gone, and the last thing they said to that person is, “I hate you.” Your character looks at the rain boots they were just about to put on, the only thing they have left now.

227. Your character stares at the figure glowing in the moonlight. Day and night, he sits high on his perch. Everyone assumes he is a scarecrow. Only he isn’t.

228. The fall carnival is bustling with excitement, vendors are selling their wares, children’s faces get painted, but something afoul is afoot through it. Someone is planning to do something terrible.

229. The police sirens ring out in the distance, and soon your character and their friends are thrown against a wall. “What happened! Tell me what happened!” The police officer barks. Your character, knees shaking, simply points to the watery bowl in the corner. They were only bobbing for apples. What has gone so wrong?

230. Your character just moved from New Mexico to New Hampshire. It’s their first time experiencing a cold, colorful fall. What activity does your character want to do first?

231. The food donation box looks so tempting. Your character hasn’t eaten all day, and since they are only in elementary *since morning* is a long time. They open a pack of crackers and scarf them down, one-by-one. The teacher catches them in the act.

232. Your character and their family decide to go on a hayride. Halfway through, one of the tires blows out. While waiting for what is supposed to be a quick repair, your character decides to explore the area. When they come back, the tractor and carriage are gone.

233. It's your character's first job working in a coffee shop. When your character opens the café, they discover a family of mice has all eaten the fall pastries. The morning rush is about to come in.

234. Your character wants to do something special with their carved pumpkin. Looking through their favorite social media app, they discover how to make a pumpkin volcano. Following the directions, your character expects bubbles of frothing foam. Instead, actual lava pours out of the pumpkin.

235. Your character and their friends are jumping around and playing with the fallen leaves. One of your friends jumps into a pile and vanishes.

236. Your character's office holds a potluck in celebration of Halloween. Your character decides to order food instead of cooking, which they pass off as their own.

Everyone loves it! So much so that your character begins to receive orders from coworkers.

237. On a cold, rainy day, your character decides to bundle up and take a nap. When they wake up, they're in a pumpkin patch. Panicked, your character runs towards a nearby truck. Seeing the keys are left inside, they get in and start the car. Backing up, they stop and scream when they look in the rearview mirror. Instead of their head, there is a pumpkin.

238. While walking through an orange and yellow forest, your character notices a child collecting pine cones in a bucket. Your character asks them what they plan on doing with all of those pinecones. The child tells them, "It's for my friend that lives in a hole." Curious, your character decides to follow them to the hole.

239. Your character is face painting for the Fall Festival. After countless leaf faces and pumpkins, a stranger requests a strange design to be painted on them. After your character is finished, the stranger grins, and everything turns pitch black.

240. Your character and their best friend are home alone. Their best friend tells them that they've never had pumpkin pie. After looking through the kitchen, the only ingredient they don't have is the pumpkin. They decide to find a substitute. What is the strangest thing that you can think of that might work?

241. Your character is reheating food in the microwave. When they take the plate out, they find that their left-over turkey meal is now a pile of candy corn. Thinking they've lost their mind, your character goes to the fridge to get some water. Instead of dispensing water, only candy corn comes out. Freaked out, your character opens up the refrigerator and the pantry only to discover *everything* is now candy corn.

242. After planting a garden earlier in the year, your character proudly harvests a multitude of veggies. Suddenly, a group of fifty or so rabbits swoop in and steal the basket. Surprised and dumbfounded, your character chases after them.

243. Your character is terrified of knives and has never carved pumpkins, but has wanted to do something fun with them. They decide to host a pumpkin painting party to enjoy the season.

244. Your character decides to pull a prank on their friends. Knowing that they'll be picking pumpkin on the local farm, your character tries on a scarecrow costume. The costume is tight and hard to get off, so they decide to go to the farm already outfitted. This prank does not go as planned. The ensemble is stuck for good, and everyone is too busy screaming to help.

245. From your character's hospital bed, they can see the leaves changing and falling. They love this time of year and reflect on memories of fall.

246. Your character makes a crockpot hot toddy batch for a get-together and an apple cider crockpot batch for their child's Kindergarten fall party. After dropping off their kid and the cluster, they come home to prepare. After your character's friends arrive, they all comment on how delicious the apple cider is.

247. After searching online, your character discovers a café that sells unusual drinks. It's in a strange location because it is in the middle of the woods, but they decide to walk over to try it out. Once inside, they notice unfamiliar patrons wearing strange symbols, their skin covered in a green tinge. Going up to the counter, they decide to try a drink called Witches Brew.

248. Your character's family wants to do something different this year and decides to decorate a Fall/Halloween tree. What decorations does your character want to use for the tree? Will the idea catch on?

249. Your character wants to dare the new corn maze. While exploring and enjoying their time, your character suddenly hears screams from the other participants. Footsteps follow, along with the noise of metal scraping against rocks.

250. Your character is babysitting. It is rainy and windy outside, so the kids have to play indoors. What Fall activities does your character do with the kids to keep them occupied?

251. Before Thanksgiving, your professor character has their class write an essay on what they are thankful for. While grading, your character stumbles on a paper that takes their breath away. How so, and in what way does it change your character's outlook on life?

252. Your character and their crush are having a bonfire party. Their friends leave the two of them alone. Once by themselves, the object of your character's affection reveals a dark secret. Does this change how your character feels?

253. At the Fall Fair, there is a pumpkin pie eating contest. Your character has always wanted to participate, but they have been too shy to do so. They decide this year that they want to give it a shot. It turns out they are incredibly good at eating pie.

254. Your character wants to start eating healthier. Unfortunately, with all the fall treats, it's been hard to get healthy snacks on the go. They decide to make some tasty fall snacks ahead of time. What does your character make? Suppose your character then creates a new business model featuring these delicious, healthy fall treats.

255. Your character just picked up a new fall hobby, crocheting. They seem to be picking it up quickly and decide to start making a hat. Once finished, your character can't stop crocheting. As hard as they try, their fingers loop through and work on a life-size version of themselves. Once finished, your character looks on with horror as the yarn doll comes to life.

256. Your character is chosen to cook the turkey for their big family dinner. Once done, your character leaves the turkey in the bag and prepares the dining room. Coming back to the kitchen, they find their dog dragging the turkey bag out. After being caught, the dog makes a run for it, the cooked bird still in their maw.

257. It's your character's first Oktoberfest. They are generally lightweight, but they decided to drink to their heart's content. After blacking out, your character wakes up in a jail cell. What happened at the festival?

Winter

Some may hate winter because of the oppressive cold. However, there is something warm about the coziness of tucking away from the elements. Whether traveling for the Holidays or avoiding inclement weather, these prompts all deal with the magic of winter.

258. A loud crash wakes your character up one frosty morning. As they cautiously head down the stairs, they are startled by a large amount of reindeer that has broken into their home. They're destroying *everything*.

259. While watching the weather report, your character hears of a snow storm coming in. A few hours later, jingle bells and flashing lights circle around your character's apartment like a tornado. Your character and their roommate look out the window to see what is going on. The snowstorm has hit, and it's brought the North Pole with it, showering the complex with Christmas lights, elf-like creatures, presents, and reindeer.

260. Your character and their rivals are going head to head in a sledding contest. On the way down, one of the sledders goes off course to throw your character off. Not wanting them to win, your character follows them into unfamiliar territory, unaware someone is watching.

261. Your character wakes up and looks out the window. Snowflakes are raining down, and your character is in awe. The shapes are so different and vibrant that they feel inspired to draw them. Which snowflake pattern draws your character in the most?

262. Your character watches their child make a snow fort. When finished, your character's child goes in. A minute later, lights shine, and music rings from the fort. Curious, your character decides to crawl in. It seems that their child has built a whole holiday world.

263. Your character decides to go ice fishing with a group of friends. After a few minutes, your character feels their catch tugging hard on the line. A humongous fish pulls your character into the water before the line breaks. Their friends rush over to help. Will your character be saved?

264. After your character's retirement, they try to find ways to occupy their time, especially during the holidays. They decide to start a sugar cookie exchange and employ their grandchildren to help. Their grandchildren have always loved eating your character's cookies but have never learned how to bake. What could go wrong?

265. After years of joining the caroling group, the leader requested that your character not join them this year. Angered by the news, your character decides to go caroling by themselves. There is a house that the group always avoided, so your character chooses this place for their first stop. Something horrifying opens the door and sucks your character right in. Curiously enough, it might be their singing that saves them.

266. During a snowstorm, your character decides to make hot chocolate from scratch to warm themselves up. They have a unique way of making it and use unusual toppings. How do they make and top their hot chocolate?

267. Your character and family want to do something new this year and decide to go shopping for a real tree instead of the artificial one they usually put up. After buying the tree, your character and family soon realize that the 7ft tall pine is too big for their modest-sized hatchback. Not wanting to exchange the tree, they try to rope it to the top of the hood—big mistake.

268. Your character decides to get away from the cold and goes on vacation. Expecting a warm, sunny beach when they land, they instead see snow patches on the runway. This can't be right. It seems they managed to get on the wrong plane.

269. Your character's parents want your character to shovel snow during the weekend for their family's visit. Your character says they will, but then busy themselves with videogames instead. Outside, someone screams. One of your character's relatives has slipped on the snow and broken a hip when they arrive.

270. Your character has always had a fondness for snow angels. They have never shared why with anyone else until they are lying on their back, arms dangled to the side, with the person they want to marry.

271. Although many plants die during the winter, your character has discovered how to keep their garden growing and flourishing. With no greenhouse or other reasonable method, your neighbors start blaming witchcraft; however, your character has something else that they use that isn't a spell. How do they do it?

272. Your character is vacationing at a Colorado resort. They develop a crush on one of the ski instructors and decide to take up lessons. It ends with a broken leg and a trip to a hospital. Does it also end in love?

273. Your character is unexpectedly snowed in without electricity or running water. They live in an area that generally never gets snow, so they are severely underprepared. They have a fireplace and other essentials that they could use to ride out the storm; however, your character has never started a fire before and relies heavily on their smartphone. How do they survive?

274. Your character and their neighborhood friends are having a snowman building contest. Some build snow animals, snow people, and some create snow creatures. After the game is over, your character and their friends notice something weird about their creations. They start moving around and making noises.

275. Your character's workplace is hosting an ugly sweater party. An array of co-workers arrive in Hanukkah and Christmas inspired sweaters. Your character's sweater, however, garners attention for the wrong reasons. They must go to HR. What is it about their outfit that is so offensive?

276. Your character's family get together is going smoothly. That is until one of your character's relatives has a little too much-spiked eggnog. Having shared a secret with them, this relative begins spilling the beans on what your character's secret is. The family looks at your character in shock and awe. What was the secret?

277. Your character has always gone overboard during the holidays for their kids. On Christmas Eve, they find a letter addressed to Santa from one of their children. Your character's child had made a list of presents for their friends that generally don't get gifts. Touched, and in a time crunch, your character decides to fulfill their child's wishlist. How do they do it?

278. A snowball fight takes place between your character and their partner. It's all fun and games until the snowballs start flying. The snowball fight creates an intense argument, in which the characters ultimately decide to end things.

279. Not being able to afford holiday lights or decorations, your character enviously decides to steal them from another neighborhood. After clearing out their first yard, the stranger's front door opens to reveal an older woman. She yells across to your character, "Would you like to come in for some hot chocolate?" What does your character do?

280. Your character finds a frozen lake to practice their ice skating routine. Woodland creatures soon gather around your character to watch the performance.

Flattered, your character finishes a challenging jump and bows. Your character swears the animals are clapping with their little paws. Your character is about to walk away when they hear one of the rabbits audibly shout, “Encore, human!”

281. Your character lied on their resume to get a holiday part-time job. Thinking that it would be easy, they say they had experience driving a horse-drawn sleigh. Their first passengers approach, and your character gets into the driver’s seat and tugs on the reins. Your character forgot to attach the horse to the sleigh, and now it is galloping away, leaping over small children and their parents.

282. Your character decides to make use of the indoor hotel hot tub. When ready to go back to your room, your character realizes too late that their towel and hotel keycard is missing. Worse still, your character cannot remember what room they are staying in.

283. One night, your character notices a stray dog huddling near their door, trying to get warm. Your character lets them in and gives the poor pooch something to eat. A few hours later, the dog barks and scratches at the door. Your character opens the door, and the dog runs out. A few hours later, the dog comes back with a few human friends.

284. Living in the American South means that "cold" is a steady 30 degrees Fahrenheit. Your character is about to travel to a place that doesn't see anything above that number. Hopefully, they remember to pack warm clothes.

285. Your character and their friends decide to make and sell snow cones using the snow on the ground. They build a display and showcase an array of syrups and sizes. What could go wrong?

286. For fun, your character fills up a spray bottle with water and food coloring and writes in the snow, "hello" on their new neighbor's snowy lawn. The next day, there is another "hello," written below with blood.

287. Your character and their child are enjoying breakfast until their child looks outside and starts crying. Your character notices that their snowman is starting to melt. What does your character do to cheer their child up?

288. Your character's hobby is gingerbread making. After spending years constructing multiple gingerbread houses, people, and towns, they want to take it up a notch. They want to build a gingerbread house to live in.

289. Your character is determined to start the new year right and complete their resolutions. They receive a journal over the holidays that promises, "Success, no matter the cost" inscribed on the front. Motivated, your character writes down everything that they want and want to do. The next day, a chain of events occurs in which everything is fulfilled. What is the cost?

290. While hiking, your character gets lost in a snow ridden pine forest. Hearing footsteps approach, your character calls out for help. Taken aback by what comes out of the thick woods, your character makes a run for it. What is chasing your character?

291. During the winter months, your character likes to give back and anonymously places gift cards and money around supermarkets and malls. One day, your character is stopped by someone that noticed them and asked your character why they are doing this. What is your character's story?

292. Seeing *The Nutcracker* is something your character has always wanted to experience but has never had the opportunity to do so. One day, your character's family decides to take them to see it. What is your character's reaction to this and the performance?

293. While vacationing near a mountain town, your character and friends decide to check out a local holiday-inspired amusement park. The park appears open and running but abandoned. Curious, they decide to split up and explore the area. Halfway through, an injured, disheveled man runs into your character's group and tells them to hide if they want to survive. Do they hide or try to find the others?

294. Your character's family is visiting from Sweden. Your character finds out that their family loves cinnamon buns and orders them from the bakery. After poking and prodding the frosting, your character's Swedish relatives lead your character to the kitchen and start showing your character how to make real Swedish cinnamon buns.

295. It is a holiday movie night, and it's your character's turn to pick the assortment of movies to watch with their friends and family. Which ones does your character pick and why?

Western Holidays

The following prompts refer to holidays in the Western world; the United States, Canada, and Latin America. Holidays like the 4th of July or *Dia De Los Muertos* are examples of holidays unique to these locales. A holiday like Christmas, for example, may have universal appeal but is celebrated differently around the world.

296. Your character is lucky enough to be watching the ball drop from a front-row seat in Times Square. In a panic, your character realizes that they are alone, and soon, everyone will be scrambling to find their own New Year's Eve kiss. *5...4...*their eyes dart around quickly*...3...2...* what happens next?

297. The New Year's baby is remarkable for both families and hospitals. A baby born on New Year's Day is supposed to bring joy and good fortune to those around them. However, what happens if this particular baby turns out to be *evil*?

298. Did you know that many Latin American cultures have a tradition surrounding New Year's eve and underwear? Tradition says that the color underwear you wear on New Year's eve will determine what kind of year you will have when you wake up. Red for romance, Yellow for wealth, White for peace, Blue for good health, Green for long life, and Pink for general harmony. What color will your character wear?

299. January 2nd is the American National Science Fiction Day. For this scenario, craft a post-New Year's tale, whether one finds new love or undergoes a career change, with a science fiction twist.

300. In many Catholic Latin American countries, January 6th is *Día de Los Reyes Magos,* also known as *Día de Los Santos Reyes,* or simply Epiphany. This is said to be the day that the Three Wise Men visited a newborn Jesus. Craft a narrative where your character is visiting a Latin American country and celebrating this holiday for the first time.

301. January 17th is considered the National Ditch New Year's Resolution Day. This is because, statistically speaking, many New Year's resolutions are forgotten by this day. Your character is determined to be different. On this day, they will keep their resolve, no matter what the cost might be.

302. Your character is celebrating President's Day at Mt. Rushmore in South Dakota. It's a fitting adventure, admiring the faces of George Washington, Thomas Jefferson, Theodore Roosevelt, and Abraham Lincoln; that is until one of the faces begins to speak in a loud, booming voice.

303. *Carnaval* is essentially a big party that happens before Ash Wednesday and Lent. In many places, the holidays include floats, parades, and outright dancing in the streets. Suppose your character is on one such float. Perhaps, the most exuberant one there is. How did they come to be there, and what experiences might they have during the parade route?

304. Mardi Gras is the day that marks the end of Carnival. Louisiana has even made it an official holiday. Your character is in one of the best places to celebrate - New Orleans. In this scenario, give them a whole night of chaos—the more unusual and strange their encounters, the better.

305. Ash Wednesday marks the beginning of Lent, which is a holiday itself marked by fasting and reflection. Traditionally, one bears the cross, in ash or a similar substance, on their forehead. While many in Western society are familiar with this practice, picture a scenario where one has no idea what is happening and is merely looking out at a sea of faces, all bearing the same mark, wearing solemn expressions.

306. As mentioned, Lent is a time of fasting and reflection, typically lasting for six weeks. It is customary to "give up" something for Lent. Some will choose to fast by forgoing meat or chocolate, while some forgo an unavoidable vice. What does your character do?

307. Is your character wearing green? Suppose that they aren't, and it is St. Patrick's Day. They should expect to get a pinch, as is customary when one isn't wearing the right color, but this time they also get so much more. They happen to be pinched by a real Leprechaun.

308. It is April Fools! You have two tasks in this prompt. In one point of view, consider what might happen if your character plays a joke on the *wrong* person, and in a different point of view, consider how the person pranked feels.

309. There are many different ways to celebrate Easter. Easter eggs can be hidden and found or filled with confetti in some cultures. Others choose the day to attend church and have a big feast. How does your character choose to celebrate this holiday?

310. *Cinco de Mayo* is far more than an excuse to drink tequila and get cheap tacos; nor is it Mexico's independence day, as many falsely believe. It commemorates Mexico's victory over the French at the Battle of Puebla on May 5th, 1862. In this scenario, have your character celebrate it sans tacos and tequila, and more authentically.

311. Envision a scenario in which your character just wants a relaxing Mother's Day but doesn't get it. Their idea of a relaxing day can include spending time with their mother, a mother figure, or having some time with their children. It could also mean that they want time away from the pressures of family life. Why is it that they do not get the day they wanted?

312. Memorial Day is a time to celebrate the sacrifice made by United States soldiers. In this scenario, craft a picture, from start to finish, from one wounded soldier's perspective. Envision how they might feel when those around them are only using the holiday as an excuse to relax or barbecue.

313. June 2nd is National Leave the Office Early Day. The thing about these "national" holidays is that few people know about them. This means that your character will have to explain to their boss why they left work two hours early.

314. On Father's Day, your character wants to give their father, or a father figure, the perfect gift. After visiting six stores, they are still short-handed. They make their way to the seventh place. Naturally, one might settle for a gift card by this point, but your character is determined to get the *perfect* gift. Why is that?

315. June 18th is International Panic Day, which is a real, but rarely thought of holiday. Your character has high anxiety and has been "celebrating" the same way every day. That is, until the actual Panic Day. Does everyone mock-panicking around them give them some validation, or does it affect their mental health even more?

316. It's *Litha*, also known as Midsummer. The longest day and the shortest night of the year. Your character is about to be transported back into time to the first celebration. How does it go?

317. July has many Independence Days. Canada is July 1st, while the United States is July 4th. Venezuela is July $5^{th,}$ and Argentina is July 9th. Choose an Independence Day and craft a narrative that explains how your character will celebrate.

318. Both Canada and the United States celebrate Labor Day. Suppose your character must work on Labor Day, and they are not exactly happy about it. What they don't know is that a surprise will happen as a result. Will they get fired? A promotion? Something else entirely?

319. September 6th is Read A Book Day. Your character, a notorious bookworm, decides to pursue some of their favorite reads. All is going well, so well that they are suddenly find themselves transported into the world *of* the book.

320. Arr Matey. September 19th is Talk Like a Pirate Day. Your character, an actual pirate, decides this might be the perfect day to steal a boat.

321. Of all the unofficial holidays, one of my personal favorites is Comic Book Day, which occurs on September 25th. Picture a scenario in which your character runs a comic book store and is about to get a rush of customers when usually they only get a handful of regulars. Are they prepared for the new influx of patrons?

322. Samhain, All Hallow's Eve, or Halloween is more than just a time to dress up in scary costumes and go Trick R' Treating. It is also a time of renewal and to remember the ancestors. Your character learns this the hard way when they offend a group of witches at this important holiday.

323. Suppose your character is celebrating Halloween in more of a commercialized way. They have already gone to a pumpkin patch, carved pumpkins, gone on a hayride, been to a few costumed parties, and now they want to find a haunted house. A real one. What could go wrong?

324. *Dia de Los Muertos* or Day of the Dead is a time to honor one's ancestors and deceased loved ones. During this time, the barrier between the land of the living and the dead are gone. Mexicans celebrate through traditional feasts, dancing, candles, flowers, and paying respect via that *ofrendas*, or altars. Your character has been invited to this celebration for the very first time. The first time since they passed that is.

325. Thanksgiving is a time for merriment, fellowship with family, and trying not to burn the house down. While your character has no problem fulfilling the first requirement, they may have inadvertently caused a massive kitchen fire.

326. In another Thanksgiving scenario, suppose your character has no one to spend the holiday with. How might they seek out warmth and companionship? It may be through a food bank, volunteering or seeking help, inviting neighbors, visiting a restaurant, or some other type of avenue.

327. While Black Friday is not a holiday per se, it is often treated as such. Your character waits outside their favorite store, eager to be one of the first people to snag a major deal. When something happens, that will make them realize that the Holidays' overcommercialization might have unintended consequences.

328. *Las Posadas* marks Mary and Joseph's search for somewhere to stay. The holiday is celebrated by Christians and Catholics alike. On this day, believers celebrate by visiting friends and family members, eating large feasts, and singing carols. Your character takes a perilous journey trying to get to a family member on this sacred day.

329. December 20th is National Ugly Sweater Day. Your character celebrates on the *wrong* day and is now sheepishly wearing the most god awful sweater during an important work meeting.

330. Your character decides to leave out milk and cookies for Santa on Christmas Eve. Of course, they don't believe that good old Saint Nick will even show up, but he does nonetheless.

331. On Christmas Day, your character finds that they have more presents under the tree than they remember before they went to bed. It isn't Santa who has come to surprise them, but someone else entirely.

332. The day after Christmas is Boxing Day for Canadians and was originally the day when employers would offer presents to employees, though now it is a day full of sales and additional time off work. Suppose your character's employer is going to celebrate the old fashioned way, with a tacky gift. Refusal by your character may mean a tense work environment.

333. It's winter solstice and also one of the longest snowstorms on record. Your character had every intention of going out and celebrating, but now they are stuck inside. How will they bring in the coming year now?

Eastern Holidays

Like with the Western Holidays section above, these Eastern Holidays are unique to Africa, Australia, and Europe. These holidays often have Old World charm with roots going back for thousands of years.

334. There are St. Patrick's Day celebrations the world over, but how does it differ in Ireland? Research a city such as Galway or Belfast and examine how they celebrate this Irish tradition. Then, write a story that includes these elements.

335. Your character is exploring the Irish countryside when they see huge fires in the distance. On closer inspection, it appears to be a series of controlled bonfires. It looks like *Bealtaine* or Mayday is taking place.

336. While staying in Ireland, your character decides to visit a Mummer festival. This is a celebration of St. Stephen's day, a national holiday. In it, men and boys often dress in straw outfits. There are lots of singing and dancing. How does your character involve themselves in the celebration?

337. *Koningsdag* or King's Day is one of the most popular holidays in the Netherlands. It was initially a celebration of Princess Wilhelmina's birthday in the 1880s. Your character is an investigative reporter exploring this holiday, talking to Dutch people dressed in orange and dancing in the streets.

338. Wine and sima (a type of mead) are flowing, floats are rolling by, and people are joyously singing and dancing. It's Walpurgis, or Vappu Day, a holiday in Finland. Your character, however, is trying to avoid the commotion. Tomorrow they have their quiet itinerary planned and do not want to participate in the revelry. Will they succeed?

339. The day is long, very long. There's very little darkness, even when it's night. Your character is a guest of honor during the St. John's celebration, indicating the arrival of Midsomer. Your character is new to these customs, and to add to the newness to them, they are asked to participate in a mock wedding with people they do not know.

340. Your character is staring at the Eiffel Tower, with red, white, and blue flags all around them. Cymbals are blaring, and people are shouting. It's Bastille Day, and the fireworks have just begun. This is the moment where they are also going to propose to their loved one. Why have they chosen to use this French holiday as their backdrop?

341. Your character has been planning this trip for months. It is the Feast of Saint Gennaro. However, when they arrive in Naples, they inadvertently lose their bag, including their phone, ID, and hotel information. Shops and businesses are typically closed for this holiday. How does your character get help?

342. The Chinese Harbin International Ice and Snow Sculpture Festival is one of the world's biggest ice festivals. On a cold January day, your character decides to visit this festival, hoping that it will elevate their mood. What has them down in the first place?

343. The New Year celebrations in China are world-famous. Write a story in which your character joins in on this holiday for the first time. Include another first for them. For instance, the first time they fall in love, they use public transport, etc.

344. Another popular Chinese holiday is the Dragon Boat Festival. This one-day celebration honors Chinese workers. While there is usually good humor and relaxation, write a scenario where a revolt is underway.

345. While visiting Taiwan, your character sees a group of people clamoring in a small cemetery. Many of them have beautiful bouquets, while others have gifts and ornaments. It's the Qingming Tomb-Sweeping Day, a time to honor the deceased.

346. How many steps does one do on an average day? How about a flight of 272 steps? This is a part of the Hindu festival Thaipusam, which includes an eight-hour procession from the Sri Mahamariamman Temple. Choose whether your character is an observer or participant and write a story that focuses on this celebration.

347. The Holi or *Dhuli* festival is known as the Hindu Festival of Love. It is a time of renewing relationships or setting to rest conflicts found within. The celebration is notable for the colored powder thrown everywhere, making a gorgeous display of love and other positive emotions. Your character and their partner is participating in the hopes that it will fix their broken marriage.

348. The Taiwan lantern festival is a time to ward off evil and disease. It is made possible by the thousands of lanterns filling the night sky. Your character, a terminally ill patient, is casting their last wish on one, hoping it might come true.

349. Your character is about to visit one of the world's most enormous water fights. The Songkran festival is a time for spring cleaning, visiting elders, but also throwing water. Suppose your character has just lost a parent and is using this festival as a way to cope, using the water as a literal renewal.

350. Your character is a huge music fan and is finally getting a chance to visit a festival that has been on their list for a long time. The Rainforest World Musical Festival is a celebration of music held against a backdrop of lush forests. How do they spend their time at the festival?

351. There have been many wars and engagements fought throughout Asia. Choose one and write a story in which your character celebrates the ending of this battle. How do they do so?

352. Your character is visiting the Daecheon beach in South Korea. They have been invited by a friend who says an "enjoyable" event will take place. It turns out it's the Boryeong Mud Festival. Things are about to get very, very dirty.

353. Your character has not been a fan of the winter season for several years, ever since a parent passed. However, to help them cope with this loss, they have decided to visit Japan for the Winter Light Festival.

Over a million LED lights are on display, as well as other festivities. Does your character find a way to find solace in this beautiful display?

354. World War II was a large-scale engagement that affected many different countries. While you may be familiar with its history, did you know that various celebrations take place globally? In Russia, Victory Day often includes watching soviet war films, a military procession, and using it as a day of remembrance. Write a historical story where a small family celebrates their holiday, having just lost a loved one to the war.

355. Many different countries have holidays set to honor those who have served and died in battle. Australia and New Zealand are no different. Commemorative festivities are held on Anzac day. Your character is a young soldier and is celebrating this holiday when they are approached by an elderly former soldier who wants only to impart wisdom to the young.

356. Your character is visiting Australia on Australia Day. Write a story that involves some of the festivities that occur on this day. Be sure to touch on the culture, both in a historical context and how modern Australians celebrate the day.

357. While visiting the countryside, your character sees massive balloons drifting upwards to the sky. Some are shaped like animals, while others are bright and colorful hot air balloons. Your character has inadvertently come upon the Canberra Balloon Spectacular.

358. Every year, on February 6th, Waitangi Day is held in New Zealand. This holiday celebrates the signing of the Treaty of Waitangi. However, this document is not without controversy. Research this and write a story from the perspective of a character that lived during this time.

359. Holidays like Christmas and Halloween have often been celebrated the world over. Choose one of these and write a story that takes place in an Eastern Hemisphere country. What is unique about these celebrations?

360. Choose an ocean at random. Now, choose a country this ocean touches. This is where your character will wash ashore. It so happens also to be a national holiday taking place.

361. Choose three holidays from three different countries. You can use some from this section or research three new ones. Write a story in which your character goes on an adventure, not only participating in each celebration but getting in various shenanigans along the way.

362. Some of the most misunderstood religious practices are Voodoo and Hoodoo. Many take elements from these without ever learning about the anthropological aspects of such practices. Suppose your character is visiting the Quidah Voodoo Festival in Ghana. They intend to write a book, but they are about to get schooled on what happens when you fail to respect the culture.

363. Every two years, the Festival of Dancing Masks takes place in Burkina Faso. Masks are usually made from grass and can be as long as six feet (two meters). It is a time for music, but also storytelling. Your character, hidden behind their mask, is going to be a silent observer.

364. Your character is looking for new inspiration for their art, be it traditional fine art, music, poetry, etc. They decide to attend the Gaborone Music and Culture Week in Botswana, which celebrates all art forms.

365. Each year thousands of wildebeests and zebras migrate between the Masai Mara and the Serengeti. This is often known as "The Great Migration." Suppose that your character is a wildlife photographer that is privy to this remarkable event.

366. Your character is about to enter a 100 km race that will take one through ancient Egyptian pyramids and other historic sights. The Pharaonic Race, which takes place in Cairo, will push your character to their limits. How do they do?

367. The Santabary Festival, which takes place in Madagascar, is centered on the rice harvest. It consists of traditional music and dance, as well as lots of eating and drinking. Write a story in which this festival goes on despite a large scale drought being imminent.

368. Many cultures have holidays that involve living sacrifice, typically a hoofed animal, as part of their celebrations. These sacrifices can be a gift to a deity, a symbolic gesture, or a precursor to a large feast. Where does your character stand on the issue? Write a story where they attend a celebration that predominately features sacrifice, causing your character to voice their opinions loudly.

369. Choose a country missing from this section. Research a holiday that takes place there. Write a story that not only incorporates this festival but also reveals something about your character. For instance, they realize they never had a sense of culture, decide to break up with their partner, etc.

370. Not all holidays are centuries or even hundreds of years old. Choose a country in the Eastern Hemisphere and thoroughly research its history and culture. Then create a new holiday for your character to celebrate.

Special Occasions

Birthdays, anniversaries, weddings; we humans love to find new reasons to have a party filled with food, fun, and laughter. These prompts all deal with unique celebrations between friends and family.

371. Your character holds a "just because" celebration and invites all of their closest friends and family. Partygoers are excited to celebrate, even if there is no reason until your character makes a stunning announcement. What is it?

372. Your character attends their friend's bachelor/bachelorette party. There, a crime takes place, but your character is sworn to secrecy. Do they tell a soul?

373. Your character is a surgeon who has been waiting on a grant that will provide additional staff and resources for their department. If they fail, many patients may die. Finally, after months of waiting, they get the news. It's double what they expected. What do they do with the excess?

374. After ten years of marriage, your character is having a divorce party. The divorce hasn't happened yet, but they are celebrating their decision with close friends. Your character's partner is unaware of the pending request, but they are about to find out. One of the attendees is about to tell them before your character does.

375. It's opening night for the largest club in town. The line is out the door, and rumor is that some well-known celebrities are inside. Your character, nameless in the sea of famous people, has somehow made it in. They are about to have a night that will change their life forever.

376. Think of a business you would love to start. Now, think of what its grand opening might look like. Write a scene in which your character is at this opening when something goes wrong.

377. It's a new beginning. Your character has purchased a new home in a city thousands of miles from where they used to live. This big move is purposeful. What are they escaping from? More importantly, who?

378. After 40 years working for the same company, your character retires. They get thrown the usual retirement party, complete with well-wishers from fellow employees longing for their exit. At this same time, the stock market crashes, and the next depression sinks in. Your character no longer has enough money to retire. What's the next step?

379. Your character is a scientist who has spent much of their adult life working on the same cure. After years of tests and sleepless nights in the lab, their research is finally complete, but the celebration takes a dramatic turn when pharmaceutical companies' offers roll in. Will they get rich or help as many people as possible?

380. Throughout our lifetime, we will have taken hundreds of tests and exams. What was your first? Write from the perspective of a child in grade school, taking and then passing their very first exam.

381. Your character opens the door to a surprise party. It isn't a birthday celebration, nor is it for their retirement, a new job, baby shower, or anything else one might expect. They have touched the lives of many through their job, and now the community is saying thanks. What occupation do they have?

382. Your character has first-day school jitters, unsure how they will be treated by others, nervous about the workload, etc. They aren't a child; instead, they are a nontraditional age students going back to school after almost two decades. How does their first day go?

383. Your character is attempting one of the most grueling marathons on Earth. It takes place through dense woods, which houses all manners of dangerous wildlife. Write a story in which your character completes this marathon, but not without several challenges.

384. Frequently, stories deal with wedding anniversaries, but the first date can be just as important. Write a story in which a couple decides to relive their very first date, several years after it has happened. What has changed from their first meeting to their life together now?

385. Your character is a teen taking their driver's license test. They know how to drive, and they would typically easily pass this test, but somehow there are both literal and figurative obstacles in their way. What are they, and how does your character overcome them?

386. It's the moment that every potential author dreams of. They have just received a book deal! This calls for a celebration. However, at the party, their publisher says that complete rewrites are necessary to make the book successful. Does your author character agree?

387. Your character has known only hardship for most of their life. They come from a dysfunctional family, where abuse and neglect were rampant. Drugs were a powerful coping mechanism. However, they are now celebrating their 5th year of recovery, and life has completely changed for them. How so?

388. Write a story in which a child performs a piece at their first musical recital. Write from the perspective of someone in the audience, who notices how sad the child becomes when they realize no one is there to see their performance. Will your character speak with the child after?

389. Your character is a teen attending their friend's Sweet 16 celebration. Suppose that, in the middle of the party, their friend's parent suddenly stops the music and loudly declares they have discovered something terrible their child has done. What is it? How does your character respond?

390. A Quinceañera celebrates a girl's 15th birthday. Dancing, good food, an intricate ceremony, and sometimes, religious additions, such as Catholicism, all occur. Research this type of celebration and write a story in which your character attends.

391. For most engagements, the couple has a celebration dinner, perhaps in an exotic or expensive location. Your character and their partner are going to do something a little more extreme. What is it?

392. There are hundreds, if not thousands, of feel-good stories of an underdog sports team winning the big game. Turn that narrative on its head. Write a story about a group that tries their hardest but still doesn't win. Somehow, with the lessons learned along the way, this loss doesn't feel like one.

393. Your character attends a baby shower for one of their closest friends. It should be a heartwarming occasion as friends and family celebrate new life. However, in the course of the shower, your character discovers a dark secret - their friend isn't pregnant.

394. Your character is witness to two people having a wedding anniversary at the table next door. From the perspective of this character, write a story about their relationship, whether good or bad. For instance, your character might observe one character talking over the other, ignoring them, etc.

395. Your character wins an award for a contest they do not remember entering. What is it, and how have they come to win the prize? Do they accept?

396. A great deal of fanfare is always on the first day of school. However, write a story that begins with a character's first day of school but ends with the last day of school. How much has changed?

397. A funeral is not typically a cause for celebration, but suppose it is in this case. Why are friends and family happy that this person is gone? For instance, the person may have been abusive, suffered through a terminal disease, etc.

398. Although your character has not been in politics for very long, they've won their first election. Now, in the middle of the campaign celebration, they are about to be privy to government secrets that they had no idea existed.

399. Your character is a first-generation college student, and they are rightfully celebrating getting their acceptance letter. They are about to be in for an even bigger surprise because soon their friends and family will tell them that they have all banded together to pay the entirety of tuition.

400. Conquering a huge fear should be a cause for celebration. For your character, it will be. Suppose your character holds a celebration marking the vanquishing of this fear. At the party, something will remind them of it. Will the phobia return?

401. Your character has been accepted into an elite program. Suppose that they had no idea that this program existed until they received an offer. It can be something outlandish, such as an invitation to join the "Men in Black" or something more serious, such as a specialized department in their company.

402. It's graduation day! Write a day-in-the-life type story in which your character gets ready, attends the celebration, and finally receives their diploma. Be sure to include all of the obstacles they have overcome to get to this point.

403. Your character has been battling cancer for many years. The odds of survival were very low. However, your character has now received the news that they are 100% cancer-free. How do they celebrate?

404. After years of working for the same company, your character receives a promotion. Not only do they make more money, but they are now in charge of ten employees. One of these underlinings is upset that they were passed over for the position and began to retaliate subtly.

405. Your character's family has owned a restaurant for generations. While the locals love it, it has never grown beyond its small corner location. All of that will change when they find themselves in a national magazine, which only reviews five-star restaurants.

406. "I object!" Your character has interrupted a wedding in progress. Everyone, including the once-happy-now-startled couple, is looking straight at your character. Why do they object to the ceremony? Will the couple still get married as a result?

407. Happy Birthday! It's your character's special day, but only they know it. Write a story in which a lonely character intends to celebrate their birthday alone, but they have the most significant celebration imaginable by the end of the piece.

Nature in All its Forms

If you want to garner some inspiration, you only need to look outside your window. Not only is nature all around us, but so are good writing ideas! You can find a great concept in rivers and mountains, trees and flowers, even the weather of the day can lead to something interesting.

The Weather

Mark Twain once wrote, "In the Spring, I have counted 136 different kinds of weather inside of 24 hours." That is one of the benefits weather offers writers. It's so temperamental it provides good fodder for story ideas.

408. Despite the countless warnings and mandatory evacuation, your character and a small group have decided to stay put and brave one of the most significant hurricanes on record. The storm surge may decimate the entire city. Will it?

409. All your character needs to do is go from point A to Point B. There they will find a small mountain checkpoint that will give them food and shelter. Getting there is easier said than done because there is a blizzard outside, and avalanches are common in the area.

410. One of the most common descriptions to describe stormy weather is "howling," as in, "howling wind." Use this as part of the opening sentence to your temperature based short story. The catch is that you should not be using this phrase to describe wind at all. Be a little more creative.

411. Due to its uncontrollable and quickly moving nature, wildfires can often be a death sentence for those unlucky enough to be in their path. Your character is a firefighter trying to gather up as many people as possible on the way out of the danger zone.

412. Your character has been warning a property developer about building a new apartment building on a mudslide prone area. After rains pour down and rivers overflow, that's what happens. A colossal mudslide causes massive destruction in the entire region.

413. A tornado has ripped through the area in a rural early 20th-century town, destroying all homes except one -

your character's. Now the townsfolk are suspiciously looking at your character, convinced that witchcraft is the culprit behind this coincidence.

414. Your character is driving down a busy road, sleet coming down in torrents. They are trying to be cautious, but the other drivers sure aren't. It does not take long before someone crashes into your character.

415. BOOM. Thunder crashes before lightning flashes. Your character's child is scared. Write a story within a story. The outer shell is the character telling this tall tale to their child. The main plot of this piece is the fantasy world itself.

416. You should always check your car's tire right after a cold snap. This is advice your character never got. Now they find themselves stranded on the side of the road in freezing temperatures. They have a spare, but they've never had to use one before.

417. Acid rain, which is precipitation containing nitrogen oxide and sulfur, is a genuine threat. While it typically causes asthma, bronchitis, and other health problems, it can also destroy crops. Suppose a new type of acid rain emerges. This one will completely decimate anything in its path.

418. It's the middle of the monsoon season, and there hasn't been a dry day in several weeks. Thankfully, no flooding has occurred. Finally, the rain stops, if only for a couple of hours. What does your character do during this dry spell?

419. What's the worst snowstorm you've ever seen? Suppose your character has never even seen snow before, and now they are going to be smack dab in the middle of a storm that will rival the one you thought of.

420. Your character has their hands behind their head, enjoying the bright sunshine on a beach in the Gulf of Mexico. The weather here can be temperamental. Just five minutes into their beach day, the rain begins to come down in a torrent.

421. Falling stars are the result of meteoroids slipping into the Earth's atmosphere. Suppose your character is amongst one of the first groups of people to witness such an event. Write a fable that explains what they think might be happening.

422. Meteors rain down on your character's town, and the people there are scared and running for cover. Your character has taken it upon themselves to get everyone to safety, even if it means sacrificing themselves.

423. Write a short story that introduces a new type of weather. Is it a unique rain type of event? Is it a new way in which snow falls? Be creative, but draw from real life for inspiration.

424. Hail can truly damage a car. Suppose a small, quick hail storm has hit a parking lot while one character is in the building. Their vehicle has damage, but no other car does. When they exit the office, they see the impact and blame another driver, unaware of the rain. A fight ensues.

425. There have been greater than average rain pours throughout history, and many world religions talk of a great flood. Suppose your character is going to live through another massive flooding event. They may even be the cause of it.

426. Rainstorms are typically relaxing and calming. For your character, storms have the opposite effect. Your character now finds themselves sitting in a therapist's office, unpacking the cause of such dread around storms.

427. Your character is witness to a strange astrological weather event. Atomic dust has been coming down from the sky, covering cars and houses alike in a peculiar green sheen. It is too soon to say what it does to human health, but it certainly can't be good.

428. Your character is knee-deep in snow, attempting to reach a destination deep in the forest. No matter how bad the weather gets, they are determined to get to this place. What is its significance? Why is your character so determined to get there?

429. It is a cloudy day, which is fitting because your character has just been kicked out of the house by their significant other. They are now walking down the street, all their belongings in a sack. The more they think about how bad things went, the angrier they become. The clouds turn darker, rain starts falling. Your character, unbeknownst to them, controls the weather.

430. Your character is the first mate on a ship halfway to its destination. After a minor bout of bad weather, the fog rolls in. It's so palpable; it's almost as if this fog is a living breathing creature. When a couple of crew members go missing, including the captain, that may just be true.

431. Living in South Florida, your character knows a thing or two about bad weather. This hurricane is different. It isn't how big or strong the storm is. It's what's IN the cyclone that is worrisome. What is it?

432. It's a bright sunny day, and your character is enjoying the weather outside. Everything seems to go well until it gets hotter. Then hotter. Your character packs up and goes home. By the time they get there, the mayor declares a national crisis.

433. After a volcano bursts, a small group must band together to survive in a world that has been overtaken by thick, clouded ash. Not only is it hard to see, but soon resources are almost nonexistent.

434. Your character is standing trial for a crime they swear they did not commit. The ruling comes down - guilty. Your character and many in the courtroom are in complete shock. Outside, a dust storm picks up. It gets stronger and stronger until the windows get blown out. Is this proof of innocence?

435. Two characters are in search of buried treasure in the wild snowy mountains. After an argument ensues, one character takes off with a compass, and the other has the map. A blizzard follows suit, and both seem to get more and more lost. Can they find each other and patch things up before it is too late?

436. At first, it was a minor drought, but after six months, riots are breaking out. Even the lakes are disappearing. Write a story in which your character gets involved in a literal water war.

437. Your character is on their way to work when a torrential downpour happens. Within minutes they are on top of their car. Others are in a similar situation. The water is becoming a river, and if they don't make it to higher ground soon, your character will get swept away.

438. During lunar eclipses, people can act out in many different strange and usual ways. Of course, this is just a myth. Or is it? Write a scenario in which your character is unaffected but escaping a group of people that have been severely affected by this "moon sickness."

439. It is a hot one, and the humidity is almost unbearable. Write a story in which your character is trying to cool themself off indoors when the air conditioner goes out. Suppose they can't seem to get anyone out to fix the problem. A few days pass, and nothing. This may get worse if they do not find any help.

440. Your character awakens to the sounds of a massive earthquake that shakes all the windows. Debris falls overhead, but thankfully your character manages to make it out alive. Some of the neighbors are not so lucky. Despite having no medical training, your character rushes to save the wounded and dying.

441. Air pollution has become a problem in both large and small cities. Your character is a researcher that is studying air pollution on a particular demographic. However, some corporate members don't want the findings released. They'll stop at nothing to ensure it won't.

442. Your character is sleepwalking but doesn't know it. Write a story where they have a strange adventure that ends with them in real life, standing outside in the morning dew; a drizzle has woken them up from their slumber.

443. Your character is a young soccer coach leading their team to victory. The rain isn't too problematic, but then lightning appears. Now, your character must round up small children amid a lightning storm.

444. Write a story in which the weather has become sentient. To control it, one has to reason with a mass of anthropomorphic clouds.

445. Write a story in which the weather changes at least three times. The key is to have the weather be a catalyst for the plot, whether causing plot points to happen or revealing a character's emotions. For instance, a character invites a partner over a sunny day, but it rains when a breakup happens, and then downright storms when one partner refuses to let the other go.

Plants

Trees can be life-giving, flowers can be deadly, and succulents can be beautiful. Plants are incredibly versatile in their purpose and in the way they look. These prompts capitalize on the abundance of diversity in the greenery that surrounds us.

446. Your character is suffering from a terrible rash caused by a bout with poison ivy. Write a short story that deals with their recovery and how they might have come into contact with the plant in the first place.

447. When you were little, were you ever told that you shouldn't eat watermelon seeds lest a watermelon grows inside you? Suppose this and other fables are real, and one child is about to find out the hard way.

448. Did you know that loofahs grow on trees? It's true! They are vegetable gourds that grow in warm climates. Write a story that has your character growing this plant and starting their own business as a result.

449. You've heard about treehouses, but what about tree-cities? Your character and their friends set out to build the first city high in the trees. If all goes well, this may be a lucrative opportunity for future developers. If all goes wrong - well, it is a *long* way down.

450. *Tiptoe through the tulips* may be lyrics to a popular song, but put your spin on this phrase. Why must one tiptoe? Are they escaping a monster? Is there an assailant in the house, and they have to sneak out? Use your imagination!

451. An unsolved, decades-old, cold case haunts your detective character. While walking past the crime scene, an old abandoned road, the missing person walks out of the forest, covered in moss but very much alive.

452. By their doctor's suggestion, your character has been rubbing Aloe Vera on a few burns they got while cooking. What they don't realize is that the plant they thought was Aloe Vera isn't at all. It's something a little more *magical*.

453. Write a short story that centers around the day-in-the-life of a landscaper. Have their backstory and a personal conflict they must overcome reveal itself throughout working on each of their client's homes.

454. Your character, and a group of friends, have snuck into a local vineyard. Not only have they eaten and drunken some of the wares, but they have also damaged some property as well. What happens when they are caught?

455. Your character is on a road trip when they discover large lavender fields on the way to their destination. They get out for a great photo op, not realizing that these are cursed lands. Anyone who steps into these fields falls into a deep, year-long sleep.

456. It's a hot summer day, but rather than grabbing a cold drink; your character has a rather inventive way to quench their thirst. They have a small array of cactuses, each with an attached spigot.

457. Your character has just gotten a job as a florist for a small shop. Write a short story that tells a story only shown through the interaction of customers. For instance, while cutting the stem off a rose, they remember a rose-covered hallway they once visited.

458. Write a fantasy in which a character is a small creature that lives in the forest. Occasionally the human population comes to them for magical herbs and healing potions. However, humans are changing.

Soon, they will see your character as something to be eradicated.

459. Your character finds themselves deep in a mushroom forest after hours of getting lost further and further in the woods. They are so painfully hungry, but only one of these types of mushrooms are edible. The rest are deadly. Do they know how to spot the difference?

460. Propagating is the act of breeding different plants together to get another species. Suppose your character is about to create a new breed of plant altogether. What might they make?

461. Your character hastily chooses a bouquet of roses from a nearby florist on their way home from work. It seems they have forgotten their own anniversary *again*. They should have listened more to the florist about what they've purchased. These are Chrysanthemums, which are usually for funerals.

462. Fruit trees are a joy to grow. They look nice, and they can provide a bounty of nourishment for many years to come. However, suppose that something or someone keeps sneaking into your character's home and stealing all the fruit.

463. Your character has figured out a way to grow only four-leaf clovers, giving them good luck whenever they want. What might happen as a result of this constant good fortune?

464. Roses have been a symbol of love for centuries. Write a story in which one's soul is contained in a single rose and is kept safe by their partner. Your character has just accidentally destroyed the rose.

465. While walking to work, your character decides to take a shortcut through a small neighborhood usually filled with random trash and raccoons. However, this is just a cover. Hidden amongst the garbage, guarded by the raccoons, is a magical, secret garden.

466. Somehow your character has gotten themselves trapped into a life-sized Venus flytrap. If they don't get out of this predicament soon, they may just end up like a fly.

467. Your character wants to have a relaxing day planting bulbs and enjoying the cooler weather. When they gather their materials, the phone rings, and your character ends up having an hour-long conversation. When they dig the holes, someone knocks on the door, and they waste another hour listening to a sales pitch. Then, another phone call. How do they cope with all these distractions?

468. Your character has decided to do something romantic for their partner. They cover the stairs and bed sheet with flower petals. Unbeknownst to them, their partner is allergic.

469. It's the annual Topiary Lover's Competition. A time when the best shrub shapers get together and out clip each other. Your character is new on the scene but is already making big waves. They've also got a secret design they've been working on for months. Will it win the judges over?

470. There have been many stories about human-eating plants, but what about human-controlled plants – that still eat other humans? Write a story about that.

471. After committing a few illegal, but relatively minor acts, your character has the most unusual punishment handed down to them. They must spend the next several weeks, pulling up weeds from outside the court.

472. Your character is a gardener for a wealthy family. Create a story in which this gardener's day-to-day life is only secondary to the family's secrets and mysteries, told from their perspective.

473. Now that your character has gotten their degree in botany, it's time for them to start on groundbreaking research. What might they want to explore in the world of plants and flowers?

474. Tillandsia, also known as air plants, get their nutrients from the air all around them. You can place them in your home to make it feel a little fresher. Suppose a character sets a new species in their house, and the plants do more than suck up nutrients. They suck the very air itself.

475. Your character sells succulents at a farmer's market. Usually, they make only a few hundred dollars, but they walk away with tens of thousands this time. What's changed?

476. No matter how you feel on the subject, drugs, whether medicinal or recreational, often come from plants. Write a short story in which your character has just made a discovery involving a drug produced from plants.

477. Your character is wrapped head to toe in thick jungle vines. The more they struggle, the more the vines tighten. How did they get into this predicament in the first place?

478. What is your favorite type of flower? What is a flower that you don't like, but others do? Write a story that deals with two characters exchanging flowers - your character gives one but receives the other.

479. The world's tallest tree, as of this writing, is 379.1 feet (115.7m). Suppose your character has set out to beat a world record - free climbing this monolith and placing their self-created flag at the top.

480. Someone has been stealing from the vegetable garden in the middle of the night! Thinking it might be a raccoon or rabbit, your character sets up a camera to determine who the culprit is. It isn't an animal at all, but their neighbor.

481. Foraging plants for food is a beneficial survival skill. Research some foraging methods and use what you learn to write a short story about a character lost in the woods, who must survive on what they find until rescued.

Waterways

Not only is the Earth composed of 71% water, but up to 60% of the human body is also h20. This organic necessity not only is the lifeblood of everyone, but it also can make for good storytelling as well.

482. Your character has been traveling across a desert for days now. Their water is close to running out, and survival does not seem likely. On the horizon, they see a shimmering oasis. Is it too good to be true?

483. Suppose that your character has gotten access to a closed aquarium after dark. What sea life do they visit, and what trouble do they get into?

484. Did you know that humankind has only explored 5% of the ocean? That means that a whopping 95% is unexplored and unknown. Your character is about to make a groundbreaking discovery. If they survive, that is.

485. While fishing in a river, your character is suddenly thrown forward by a tug on the line. This is bigger than anything they've ever caught before and then some! Your character manages to haul the fish in, only it isn't a fish. It is a sea serpent.

486. Your character is having a peaceful morning, sketching beavers busy building their dam. Suddenly, the beavers begin to cry out, pushing against each other in their attempt to run away from something. That's when the dam breaks, destroyed by giant waves.

487. What is it like inside a water bubble? Write a story that answers this question—the more creative, the better. For instance, your character may get shrunken by a scientist and trapped inside a bubble.

488. Behind your character's house is a small creek that eventually feeds into the ocean. It is not uncommon for them to find a small array of fish, turtles, and occasional snakes. This time they see a suitcase with stacks of cash in it.

489. A tributary is a river or stream that flows into an even larger river or lake. Your character is floating on a raft on one such body of water when they fall asleep. When they wake up, they aren't on a river at all nor a lake. They are in a completely different world entirely.

490. Your character is knee-deep in the swamp, trap in hand. Their family has lived off this land for almost a hundred years. Write a story that focuses on the day in the life of this character.

491. One of the biggest dangers of flooding, aside from the water itself, is what could be lurking in the water. Snakes, insects, and miscellaneous debris can create a considerable hazard. Your character is trying to get from point A to point B, all while avoiding these dangers.

492. Your character has decided to throw a pool party for their 18th birthday. On the day of the party, not one friend shows up. They can't seem to find their parents either. Where is everyone?

493. An estuary is where the river mouth meets the ocean. Your character and their child are exploring this area when tragedy strikes. What happens? Write a short story that deals with this character's grief and regrets.

494. Your character has booked a stay on the lake as part of their vacation away from busy city life. While they are having their morning coffee, someone shouts nearby. They rush outside to find that something terrible has happened in the lake. Not only does this disrupt your character's peace, but soon they are blamed for the incident.

495. "Open up now!" Your character is startled to hear banging on their door. They are even more surprised to see their apartment's maintenance team ready to tear out much of the floor. Your character's shower is flooding the apartment below. How do they cope with this unfortunate news?

496. When most people come into a large sum of money, they want to pay off all their debts or treat themselves to a new car or house. Your character buys an island. They fail to realize upon purchase that there are already occupants on this "little slice of heaven," and these islanders are not very happy about the sale.

497. While picnicking in a meadow, your character and their partner hear cries coming from a nearby well. They investigate to find a child trapped below. By the time they summon the police, the child is gone. Stranger still, the police officer tells of a cold case related to the area- of a lost child more than 50 years ago.

498. Do you know where your drinking water comes from? Research the source of your water, usually a type of reservoir, and then write a story that takes place at that locale.

499. Your character is having a fountain installed in the backyard of the home they are selling. It's beautiful and instantly increases property value. That is until the future owner stays the night. At night whispers are heard.

500. With climate change issues rising, your character has decided to buy several water tanks to store on their land. It was a smart investment, especially after a drought occurs. Now, once friendly neighbors are trying to force their way into your character's home and property.

501. Your character is a small child gleefully jumping into rain puddles on the way home from school. They find a huge one and lunge forward. They don't hit solid ground. Instead, they jump through the puddle and come out into an underwater world.

502. Your character works at a local marina. They have always dreamed of setting sail themselves. They're finally going to get their chance when someone gives them an unexpected gift – their very own ship.

503. Many coastal highways go for miles over the ocean. Suppose your character is stuck on one of these highways because they've run out of gas. There is no station within walking distance. However, they have a boat; they just have to manage to get it into the water to get help.

504. For generations, your character's family has gotten their drinking water from a nearby spring. Ever since a billion-dollar corporation has moved in, the water has tasted *strange*. It's up to your character to find out what's going on.

505. On their 16th birthday, your character discovers they have a most unusual talent. They can control water, but only 1 liter of it. What do they do with this newfound power?

506. Your character has been invited by their significant other to take a romantic boat trip down a canal. Your character braces themselves for what they believe will be a marriage proposal, but a breakup occurs by the end of the journey instead. What went wrong?

507. Take a mundane water-related activity, such as watering plants or walking in the rain, and add unexpected conflict to it. For instance, the plants are man-eating, or when walking in the shower, one stumbles across a strange creature.

508. Write a story in which a character is fishing in the middle of the ocean. They only catch small fishes, then medium size fishes, and finally, full-blown sharks. Have some internal discovery take place alongside these catches. For instance, an imploding marriage, their sexuality, something they don't like about themselves, a toxic friendship, etc.

509. Your character is alone on a glacier, drifting out further and further to sea. How did they manage to get into this predicament? How will they survive until help arrives?

510. Your character is a scientist that has been called to study a small pond. This pond seems relatively normal, except that it has become a portal to another dimension.

511. Write a story that includes at least three different water types that grow either bigger or smaller. For instance, the beginning of your account might see your character playing in a small stream, then a river, and finally, the ocean.

Geological Foundations

cliffs, caves, and rocks in general, are the focus of these prompts. While it may *seem* like not much might happen in these areas, this section will prove differently.

512. After a huge thunderstorm, a farmer goes to check on the crops. Sadly, there is so much soil erosion that this year's harvest may be nonexistent. Your character, an ecological advisor, has been called on to help save the day.

513. While on a road trip, your character hits a valley with mountains on either side. It is about to be a very rocky road when an avalanche occurs out of the blue.

514. Your character is on vacation in Washington State, visiting some of the historical landmarks. This will be a vacation of a lifetime because Mount Saint Helens is about to erupt again. This time, it's going to be the deadliest and most economically destructive, topping all other records.

515. Rimstone dams are notable for their calcareous deposits, which act as a barrier to springs. Your character is studying one up close and personal. Write a narrative in which they find something unexpected.

516. Your character is a contractor installing a new granite countertop in a customer's kitchen. The customer is the one who ordered the parts. When the contractor unwraps them, they see that it isn't granite at all. It's a type of rock your character has never seen before.

517. Your character is a hiker traversing the Appalachian mountains. While going down a particularly rough trail, they hear small groans coming from a ravine down below. Peering over, they can just make out the top of someone's head and the mangled wreckage of a car around them.

518. As a property developer, your character often looks at a piece of land and sees its potential. However, this time they must evaluate hundreds of acres of limestone that the customer wants to turn into something "amazing." What could they possibly do with this area?

519. Salt marshes are areas in which the nearby ocean often ebbs and flows with sand. Your character has been trapped for hours now, and help does not seem to be on the way. How did they get stuck in the marshes, to begin with?

520. Underneath your character's feet, tectonic plates are shifting. This means an earthquake is imminent. Write a narrative that begins with a typical week for your character, primarily focusing on day-to-day stresses. End the story with the earthquake and its aftermath. Write in a way that makes their original woes seem trivial by comparison.

521. Your character is standing on the edge of a cliff. They have created what they call "human wings" and are ready to test them out. Will this work, or are they going to fall straight into the water below?

522. Your character is knee-deep in thick mud, bent over and looking for something. What are they looking for? Further, why would this missing item be in the mudflats of all places?

523. Spelunking refers to exploring wild cave systems. This can be extremely dangerous as there is little to no help available should someone get stuck or injured. Your character is spelunking for the first time and manages to lose sight of the rest of the crew.

524. Mt. Rushmore is an iconic South Dakota landmark. Your character is visiting this historic site when the unexpected happens. The stone presidential faces are coming down - right over where your character is standing.

525. The townspeople all whisper about your character, calling them a hermit or a recluse. For years, your character has been the talk of the town. They've attended galas, soirees and lived the high life. All that changed since they've retreated into the mountains.

526. Your character is one of the first responders called in weeks after a volcano erupts. They stand on the cooled magma, take a deep breath, and survey the devastation, which is greater than even they suspected.

527. Research the kind of rocks and minerals you might find at your favorite vacation spot, be it a beach, hiking trail, or countryside house. Write a narrative in which a parent is teaching their child about the environment and its wonders.

528. Your character is a movie star, working on a new film in the Andes. This is the first time they've been to South America. How do they enjoy the mountain range and its people? What kind of conflict might arise from this change in scenery?

529. Giant worms in dunes? We have heard it before, but create your spin on this classic sci-fi trope. Write about a small town attacked or researchers training these monstrosities. Perhaps mix both. Get creative!

530. Your character is a photographer taking pictures of stunning cave columns deep underground. The guide they are with suddenly has a massive heart attack, leaving them alone and in the dark. Your character must find a way to pull their traveling companion to the surface, navigating the treacherous environment.

531. "Come on! You can do it!" Your character's partner calls out from the other side. Your character stands on the pier, overlooking the rocky path that leads to a small restaurant on the ocean. Waves gently waft over the sides. It should seem like a simple task, but your character has never been sure-footed. Do they make their way across to their love?

532. What might the center of the Earth look like? Of course, there has been at least one classic story tackling this very question, but put your spin on it. You may want to ignore the science for this and go straight for a genre with fewer limitations.

533. Your character works deep in an underground mine, toiling away in the shaft from morning until night. Their days are tedious, long, and challenging, but never changing. This time, something happens that shakes everyone to their core. The mine collapses.

534. One day, the lake near your character's house suddenly vanishes, leaving a dry bed in its wake. There's no explaining this strange phenomenon.

535. Write a story in which your character witnesses the forming of Pangea. No, no humans, or human descendants, were in existence during this time. Thus, it will require some creativity—time travel, a made-up species that was, wormhole, etc.

536. Your character is visiting the grand canyon for the first time. They first explore the same tourist traps as everyone else, camera at the ready for photo-ops. Then, a stranger comes up to them and mentions something about a lost treasure? Will your character take the journey?

537. Stalagmites jut out from the floor of a cave, while stalactites hang down from the top. Your character is studying both as they explore a cavern near the home they just bought. The realtor did not mention this came with the property, so this is a surprise. An even bigger one waits if the character dares to go further.

538. What does the inside of a volcano look like? Besides being very hot. Your character is about to find out because a new suit has been invented that can withstand almost any threshold of heat. What do they find down there?

539. Your character is a prisoner working in a rock quarry, struggling against the hot blazing sun. Someone is about to plan an escape, and your character is about to join in.

540. Write a narrative in which one character stands in the ruins of Machu Picchu, and another stands in the same place - thousands of years earlier. The only constant is the surrounding rocks and scenery. How do past and present link these characters?

Other Ecosystems

The world contains more than just rivers and valleys. These prompts deal with all kinds of ecosystems, from human-created biomes to hidden forests.

541. Your character meanders through the grasslands, attempting to find a gas station after their vehicle runs out. Already, they are upset because they made such a grave error. Their day is about to get worse when they unwittingly step into a snake den.

542. After a worldwide disaster strikes, your character finds themselves in the middle of an apocalypse. Just a few days before, your character knew where everything was. Now, it's hard even to find their own house amongst the rubble. By two months, it is a jungle out there. Literally!

543. Your character has been told there is a swamp witch deep in the bayou. Against all warning, they set off, hoping to have their mysterious ailment cured. What is this strange affliction, and further, will they make it to the witch at all, or will they succumb to the whims of the environment?

544. Your character is a soldier stationed in a desert country. They are left stranded after an encounter with an enemy. Now, they must choose between braving the wilderness and trying to find their group or seeking help from the citizens whose lands they have been occupying for almost a year.

545. Your character is a farmer who now stands in the middle of a crop field. "It happened. I swear it did!" The gathered audience, members of your character's community, begin to whisper amongst themselves.

Your character stands firm that there were ufos last night. Were there?

546. Your character has created a biodome that can mimic Earth's environment. Now it is time to test out the invention. Your character will need to live alone in this closed environment for one year; otherwise, they lose all funding. What could go wrong?

547. Chaparral is vegetation that consists of shrubs, bushes, and small trees. It is typically found in areas that have hot, dry summers and cold, wet winters. Suppose your character is exploring this area and discovers something hidden. What is it, and what do they do about it?

548. You may be familiar with most creatures in the savanna - lions, tigers, cheetahs, etc. Write a narrative that deals with some of the less notorious animals within this environment. Remember to do your research and choose animals that others would not immediately think of.

549. Your character has just bought a house in the hills, were not that many townspeople dare to go. Your character originally purchased the land to keep away from others, but now, with creepy things happening all around them, human companionship is all they want—Hopefully, of the living variety.

550. Would you consider an urban environment to be a type of ecosystem? In what ways can it be? Write a short story that focuses on an environment with no land and plenty of concrete.

551. It is a snow day, and your character couldn't be happier. However, the snow keeps falling and falling. Soon they are trapped inside their home with little to no resources. The weather says that this is unprecedented. There is simply no telling when the snow will let up. How does your character survive?

552. Your character is deep in a boreal forest in northern Canada. They do not remember how they got here but only remember flashes of a life far from where they are now. The key to their survival is to remember who they are and how they got here in the first place.

553. The Amazon rainforest is one of the most famous environments of all. Set a story here, but make it a two-part perspective. First, write from the point of view of someone that lives here. You can be extra creative and make it an animal or plant species. Then, write it from the perspective of someone who gets lost. End the story from either perspective.

554. Your character is gathering seashells on the beach when a strangely carved box washes ashore. What are the contents of this odd find? What does your character do next?

555. While on a walk in a new city, your character discovers a hidden valley. This place isn't just remarkable because of the abundance of natural edible plants, but also the amount of ruins leftover from an up-until-now undiscovered ancient civilization.

556. Research a nearby national park in your area. Focus on the animals and plants that live there and any laws and requirements affecting visitors. Write a scene in which someone breaks these rules, and your character is a witness.

557. Your character is a tribesman in pre-1700s North America. While hunting on plains, they see a visitor with skin like the moon. Write an alternate history narrative about an indigenous tribe and how an encounter with outsiders could have gone.

558. Burying friends or family members into the sand is often a favorite pastime of going to the beach. Suppose your character lets a child do just that, only to have the child run off and forget about them.

559. Your character is a top researcher at a base stationed in Antarctica. They soon get strange signals from another world. Then, the aliens show up. No one is around for thousands of miles, and it is up to this small crew to see what these strange visitors want.

560. Your character is visiting the Florida everglades as part of their exploration of the state. It is supposed to be a short trip before they continue to up to Miami. However, they never make it that far. What happens?

561. Your character finds a rabbit warren on their property but leaves it undisturbed. The next thing they know, there is a whole colony of bunnies, with more on the way.

562. Your character has snuck into the garden of a mansion so that they could pick a few pretty flowers for a loved one. However, they now find themselves running past different statues, ponds, and hedges. The more they run, the more lost they become inside this elaborate labyrinth.

563. It is a warm day, and your character is cutting the shrubbery in their yard. Suddenly, they have a massive heart attack. Write a story that deals solely with them waiting for help surrounded by plant clippings, above them a burning hot sun.

564. The smell is sharp, acidic even. Surrounding your character is the still-smoking ruin of over 100 acres of trees. Your character continues to move through the wreckage. What are they looking for? Will they find it?

565. Your character has taken the lead in building a community garden. It is one of the first urban green spaces in the area. Right before harvest, your character finds out that someone has stolen all of the vegetables. Who might be behind such a selfish act?

566. The hose is tangled, and when your character fixes the problem, the water turns off. When your character finishes raking the leaves, the dog runs through them. Include these and other mishaps in a story about your character's eventful morning working on their lawn.

567. The tundra can be a cold and unforgiving place, but not for your character. In this scenario, your character is living quite well in this arctic wasteland. It is the outside world that should be careful - of them.

568. Your character is a part of a small group of anarchists who live "off the grid" in a remote forest location. After years away from modern life, your character is starting to miss it. However, the group isn't too happy to let your character just walk back to civilization.

569. After a drunken night on the town, your character wakes up surrounded by what looks like large pieces of hay. Next to them are three large spheres, almost as tall as them. One of the round objects begins to move. With horror, your character realizes that these are eggs! They are inside a giant bird's nest, and one of the chicks is about to hatch.

570. Fire ants are found in subtropical regions and if you find one, turn the other way. Their bites hurt, and these insects are relentless. Use an ant nest as a catalyst for your story. You can have a character discover a mound or use the ants more abstractly.

571. Your character has lived in a series of treehouses all of their life, surrounded by relatives and friends. Now, outsiders discover this tree-dwelling population. For the first time, your character hears that other families don't live like this. How do they react?

572. First, choose an ecosystem at random. Then, select two other ecosystems from this list. Combine elements of all of these to create your unique setting and world. Write a story that takes place there.

Emotions, Memory, and Things Unseen.

All characters should have depth. After all, a two-dimensional character is easily forgettable, but a three-dimensional character is real enough to cast its own shadow. This section deals with the core emotions and events that make up a character. You can use these prompts as a way to better flesh out your character or as a way to put them in new, exciting scenarios.

Positive Emotions

The good moments in our lives are what make up the most long-lasting and warmest memories. That is not to say that trials do not exist within this moment, but the focus on these prompts should be to give readers a feel-good, happy end to whatever situation one might find themselves in.

573. Your character's significant other has been in quite a playful mood lately. Light teasing, making silly faces, and random acts of juggling have been a common occurrence. Your character begins to grow suspicious. Do they have a reason to be?

574. Your character is feeling quite optimistic. Although they have had a hard life, it seems their future is bright and promising. What are they looking forward to the most? How do they achieve this goal?

575. What do you use for creative inspiration? Friends, other writers, writing prompt books? Suppose your character has a literal muse. A creature that guides their hand, whether it's sculptures, paintings, writing, music, etc. The creature vanishes at the point of tremendous success. Can your character continue without this fantastical helper?

576. All their life, your character has never felt loved. Not by friends and certainly not by their family. However, they are a profoundly empathetic person whose compassion knows no bounds. They are about to be significantly rewarded for all of their good deeds.

577. In this scenario, suppose your character has just survived a horrible car crash that has killed all other passengers. They don't know this yet. Write a narrative in which your character thinks of all the things they are thankful for and how lucky they are. End the story with them receiving the news. The challenge is to make this story lighthearted and hopeful.

578. You can conceptualize the feeling of warmth in many different ways. For example, warmth can be the physical feeling when one sits by the fireplace on a cold winter day or the emotion that arises when one hugs their parents after a horrible breakup. Write a story that deals with your interpretation.

579. Your character has found a four-leaf clover, but there is a catch - the luck doesn't affect them. Instead, it affects everyone around them. Do they use this strange gift for others, or do they still find some way to benefit themselves?

580. Your character is the world's most foremost authority on art, and they often get called in to weigh in on whether or not certain pieces are forgeries. One day, they buy a famous work of art, but It is fake! If they pursue the forger, they will lose all credibility. If they don't, they will lose millions.

581. One of the words often used to describe your character is patience. Friends, family, coworkers, and often strangers will say that your character has a heart of glass and does whatever it takes to help others. But, their patience is starting to run thin.

Write about something that will truly test the bounds of your character's kindness.

582. After an eight-hour mountain climb, your character reaches the fountain of youth. They drink the elixir and immediately feel purified. They won't age, but that doesn't mean they cannot succumb to death in other ways.

583. Murphy's law states that "Anything that can go wrong, will go wrong." Your character starts with a perfect day, but a dramatic turn happens in the evening proving this adage correct. How will they cope when things suddenly go downhill?

584. Your confident character never backs down from a dare. However, this time they accept a dare that will have dangerous consequences.

585. After an archaeological discovery, your character has earned the respect of their colleagues and the academic community at large. The praises are short-lived because an ancient virus has also been unleashed.

586. Your character tries to ignore the banging noises coming from the apartment next door. At first, it is annoying and only slightly distracting. Then the banging escalates. It turns out the noises are from a burglary in progress. Your character's relaxing evening may get a little less comfortable.

587. Being a parent is such a wonderful feeling. Your character loves their new baby, but there's a catch. This isn't their child. Whose is it?

588. "You can do this!" "You're stronger than you think!" "The only person who is holding you back is you!" These are the phrases uttered by the flight instructor in front of your character. Your character felt pretty daring when they agreed to jump out of an airplane, and now they aren't so sure. Are they going to go through with it?

589. It's a full day of pampering and revitalization. Your character has been looking forward to this spa day. However, things do not go according to plan because soon, they find themselves lost and naked, trying to look for the sauna. How did this happen?

590. Choose a movement from the 1960s, such as the Women's Rights Movement. Suppose your character is a champion for this social cause and is about to change the world forever.

591. Your character is having a pleasant afternoon stroll in the woods when they come across an injured deer. Write a story in which they not only help this unfortunate animal but form an unbreakable bond as well.

592. Being in love is a beautiful feeling. Your character is inspired to write the sweetest poetry, paint the most vivid pictures, and sing the most wonderful songs. Too bad; it is unrequited love.

593. Your character is excited about a brand new book they are going to read. It has been years since the author released the last book in the series, and the preorder has finally come in. No matter how hard they try, however, your character cannot find time to dig in. It seems something or someone always gets in their way. Sometimes literally.

594. Being neat and tidy is often seen as an admirable trait. Further, it can be an excellent feeling to work in a pleasant, clean environment. At least that's the way your character sees it. They soon get a roommate that is the exact opposite. The two undoubtedly bump heads when the dishes pile up, dust mites go unnoticed, and someone misses the toilet too often.

595. Your character has had high anxiety and depression most of their life. After having the right kind of treatment, they have gotten the positive tools to help them on life's journey. Now they are determined to help others. How do they accomplish this inspiring goal?

596. Your character finds a penny on the ground. Later, they find a four-life clover before someone gifts them a horseshoe. Then a ladybug lands on them. These are all signs that your character is about to have the luckiest day imaginable.

597. Out in the middle of the ocean, drifting on a sailboat, all seems right with the world. That is until your character's peace is broken by a loud shrill. What is causing the noise, and can your character get back to solace?

598. At the nursing home where your character works, there is no shortage of bad moments. However, your character sees only the positive and handles each case with the most extraordinary tenderness. Write a scene that follows your character as they attend to a dying patient. Despite the sadness, find a way to make the moment uplifting.

599. Your character is quite academic and always eager to learn. They have excelled throughout grade school and high school, and now they will be one of the youngest people to ever go to college. How does this transition affect them? Does being so smart have its drawbacks?

600. Your character is friendly and chipper to everyone they meet, warming up even the rudest individual. This time, however, while boarding the subway, they run into someone who is downright cold. No matter how hard they try, your character simply can't seem to get through to this sourpuss.

601. Self-reliance is a very positive emotion. Show this through a character living on their own for the first time. Write a story that deals with their daily struggles. For example, you can include a scene of them getting the electricity set up or dealing with a leaky roof.

602. Your character has just been proposed to, and they've said yes! Their excitement is short-lived when someone alerts them of some hidden secret their fiancé has. What is it? Do their wedding plans fall through?

603. Are you content in your life? Is your character? Write a story that challenges what your character thinks being 'content' means. For instance, if they are happily married, incorporate betrayal. If they have a dream job, have a corporate scandal happen.

604. Sometimes it's good to get a little silly. As a professional children's birthday clown, your character spends much of their time making others laugh. However, underneath it all, they do not have much to laugh about. Write a story that delves into this character's life and woes.

605. Write a scenario in which your character has been clean and sober for precisely one year. How do they celebrate? Include any temptations that might arise and how they handle these now. For a more significant challenge, transition the past and present together.

606. Your character is motivated to tackle everything on their to-do list, no matter how hard or time-consuming. Write a comedy of errors in which your character has to overcome the most bizarre situations to get this list done.

607. Your character is their parents' favorite child. Of course, no one says it out loud, but it happens in subtle ways. In what ways is favoritism shown, and how do your characters' siblings cope? How does your character feel?

Negative Emotions

We can't be happy all the time, and neither can your characters. These prompts all deal with the emotions that we often hide. They may not be pleasant, but conflict always makes for a good story.

608. Your character is constantly jealous; of their siblings, friends, classmates, and anybody who has something your character doesn't. Where does their envious nature stem from? Can anything curb this ugly emotion?

609. Doubt can be a compelling emotion. It can cause a person to fail even before trying. Your character is grappling with extreme doubts after receiving a scholarship to an arts program of their choice. Write a narrative in which they cope with this doubt and go on to become extremely successful.

610. Your character works at a nursing home where sadness and lack of hope run rampant. Many times, it's because patients have regrets or fading memories. Sometimes both. Your character is tasked with putting on a large scale event to elevate both staff and patient spirits.

611. Your character has done something that they knew was wrong, but they did so anyway. Now a great big cloud of shame is hanging over them. What is this atrocious act they have committed? What happens if someone else finds out?

612. "Is someone there?" Your character waits but doesn't get a response. They take a few more steps, eager to get back inside to the safety of their house. They could have sworn they heard someone outside—Leafs crunch behind them. Your character tries to swallow their fear. Someone is *definitely* lurking around.

613. A well of despair has built up around your character after they lose a close family member. Life doesn't seem bright and shiny like it once did. Then, their family member shows up as a ghost, encouraging your character to find happiness even when things look grim.

614. After being picked last for every game, your character has built up a great deal of resentment for the star player. They plan out a prank that is going to show everyone who the real MVP should be. The plan not only fails, but it backfires completely.

615. Your character grew up in a religious family taught to hate others, whether because of sexuality or skin color. Since childhood, your character has been in picket lines, always told to smile while holding their sign and shouting horrible slurs at others. One day they have a complete change of heart. What has turned their hatred into empathy?

616. Your character is a medical professor at the frontline of a global pandemic. They are *exhausted*. It isn't just the increasing influx of patients, making them so tired. It is also the fact that the majority of the populace is carrying on as if nothing has happened.

617. The world seems to be getting bleaker, and your character's apathy is increasing. When all hope seems lost, they run into someone that gives them a reason to explore the possibilities that remain.

618. As a judge, it's your character's job to be a little judgemental. However, how much is bias, how much is intuition, and how much is going by the rule of law. In this narrative, follow your character as they see a string of cases with complex issues.

619. Your character has a million things to do today. An errand to the grocery store, getting their car in the shop, dealing with a fraudulent transaction, and the list goes on. Write a story in which your character goes through an overwhelming and frustrating day, but something extraordinary happens in the end.

620. Compared to others their age, your character feels woefully inadequate. They decide to do something harmful to help themselves. For instance, they stop eating if they want to lose weight or take pills to gain muscle. Craft a narrative in which the character, as well as the audience, learns about self-acceptance.

621. Your character tries hard to ignore the kicks coming from the child behind them. They've already asked the kid's parents to keep the child still since it's a long flight, but this has been to no avail. Then, the worst happens. The plane goes down. Now it's up to your character to protect the child, the only other survivor before help comes.

622. When the bombs begin to drop on your character's city, they feel powerless to protect the people they love. However, it is in the aftermath that they find their true calling.

623. After a great night on the town, your character comes home and is utterly horrified. Someone has broken into their apartment! One of their best friends comes over, helps them clean up the mess, and loans them some money to help them get back on their feet. Weeks go by, and some sense of normalcy returns. That is until they find out their friend committed the burglary.

624. Your character has had trouble concentrating at work lately. While they have had some rough weeks before and many bad days, they've never been this unfocused. After getting a test from the doctor, they locate the problem's source—a brain tumor.

625. Your character arrives at the election party feeling motivated and energetic. Four more years! However, by the end of the night, they leave the campaign office disillusioned. What information did they receive to change their views on the president?

626. Your character has become numb to all the woes in the world. No one talks to each other anymore, and when they do, people are rude and ugly. Things are looking bleak. Your character decides it's time for a change. They choose to spread joy wherever they can. Where do they start?

627. Your character wins a billion dollars overnight. Now they can do whatever they want. Houses. Cars. They can even buy an island if they so choose. But can money buy happiness?

628. There are no written instructions anywhere! Just pictures. Your character has been trying to build a basic bookshelf for three hours, and they haven't even gotten the sides connected. As their frustration mounts, so do their resolve. Write a comical story that deals with building this one piece of furniture.

629. Your character has been trying everything under the sun to combat their negative feelings; yoga, healthy eating, play therapy, acupuncture, etc. They find a new strange method; a company promises to erase all negative emotions from their brain entirely. Will they try it out?

630. Your character has an upset stomach. It's nothing major, probably something they ate. However, they are currently waiting for the interviewer to make their way into the room. This job could be a significant career changer. Their stomach gurgles and then gurgles even louder. Uh oh....

631. What is your biggest regret? Whatever it is, use this scenario as something that your character is facing in a story. Would they have chosen the same thing?

632. Negative feelings do not happen in a vacuum. Often, they stem from an inciting incident. Write out an inciting experience for your character, but do not let the audience know that this is. Use dialogue and context clues to underline what is going on.

633. Your character has always done what their parents tell them to do, even though it directly contrasts to what your character wants. Finally, they will go their own way, even if it means disapproval. How does this work out for your character?

634. Your character wakes up in a dark room, with only a small collection of objects around them. The items are completely random. For instance, you can use things like a bowling ball, carrot, matchbox with no matches, etc. Amongst the brick brack, a note reads: *Confused? Maybe something in here will help you get out of this room. Make it out, and I will tell you who I am.*

635. One of the most horrifying feelings imaginable is a personal violation. This can manifest in many different ways. Write a scenario in which a character has their trust taken away, loses a part of themselves as a result, but perseveres regardless.

636. Choose something that your character is passionate about, such as a social justice cause. Now write counter-arguments to this issue. Have another character voice these opinions to your character in the most disruptive and demeaning way possible. How does your character react?

637. Craft a scenario that is a dream within a dream. Your character has been dealing with horrible depression, causing them to sleep for hours at a time. Imagine a scenario in which they get a chance to battle their inner demons within a dream sequence, the results of which can affect their waking life.

638. It has been several years, and your character still misses a deceased loved one. There's an intense nagging feeling that tells them something about their loved one's death seems off. Then one day, they find a clue that proves what they have been guessing all along – their loved one did not die by accident!

639. "Move it or lose it!" Your character barks at the person in front of them. The customer, flushed, hurries up with their coffee order, quick to get out of your character's way. No matter what they are doing, your character is notoriously impatient. Someone who has been watching the display is about to teach them a lesson.

640. Your character is in excruciating pain after they plummet four stories. They might have broken bones, definitely bruising and swelling, but hopefully no internal damage. They look up, dazed and confused. The person who pushed them smiles and walks away. Why did this person commit this horrible act against your character?

641. The child balls up their little fists and slams them down on the counter. "More!" Their parents have already given this child everything they've ever wanted. Your character witnesses this tantrum, escalating with each refusal. Do they decide to step in?

642. Your character is turning green with envy, Literally! One day they wake up with green skin. For now, it's a light shade of green, hardly noticeable. It isn't until they turn a deep forest green that they realize that, for every time they complain about what they do not have, their skin darkens.

643. After the accident, your character feels tremendous guilt. So much so that this feeling manifests itself into a real, tangible creature. What was the accident? Why do they feel guilty about it? Will this creature ever be stopped?

The Future

What might happen in 200 years? In 1,000? What about 20,000? The future is a source of inspiration for many fiction writers because it draws from humanity's sense of exploration and quest for knowledge.

644. Your character runs one of the first flying car dealerships in the world. People come from other countries just to get a new model. Then the customers stop coming entirely. It seems a new competitor has opened up. Your character has to take the flying car concept and make that even more innovative.

645. In the future, there is no more disease. With a growing population and resources hoarded by only a few, scientists work on the deadliest pathogen of all in an attempt to curb the population. However, are these scientists pinpointing the wrong problem for the lack of food? Your character is about to find out.

646. By now, going from galaxy to galaxy is as easy as booking a cruise. Space exploration has become nothing more than yet another tourist market. New technology, however, is going to change all this. What could be next?

647. Dogs. Cats. Birds. Snakes. Hamsters. There are many common pets, but suppose in the future a new species is created. This one will become instantly popular amongst children and adults alike. What is this new pet? Further, what are the consequences of making it?

648. What do you do for fun? Video games, social media, watching television, or something else? What might people in the future do for amusement? Write a scenario that explores both the positives and negatives of this new amusement.

649. One of the biggest challenges that will come out of the future is finding renewable resources. Wind, solar, etc., are all sustainable resources, but what if there is another? Write about a recently discovered energy source that the world has never heard of before.

650. In a similar vein, write about a character that wants to steal this energy source for themselves. The course of the story is the attempt, but by the end of it, create some situation in which they have a change of heart.

651. Your character wakes up in a hospital. The last thing they remember is getting in a major car accident. Now, they find themselves signing forms they don't quite understand. In a week, they will be a cyborg.

652. You can now create practically anything with a 3d printer and the right blueprint. This may not be a good thing. Your character is a detective that has been put in charge of tracking down a terrorist group that is 3d printing weapons and selling them on the black market.

653. You may be familiar with the hundreds of mobile phone apps that can change the appearance of your face. Some will give you silly hats and glasses, while others will show you what you would look like when you are older or gender-swapped. Suppose that these apps are used to steal your identity.

654. Your character has access to antigravity boots that they have been using to break into highrise buildings. There they take everything from money to corporate secrets. In the middle of one such endeavor, the boots suddenly stop working.

655. Your character has just invented x-ray vision. At first, they were only going to sell the technology to the highest bidder, but then they discover a more noble cause – using these glasses to look at a person's organs, offering a low-cost cancer screening tool.

656. What will the military be like in the future? You can get political in this piece if you choose, but the primary focus should be on whether or not the future is more of a utopia or dystopia and what new weapon technologies might arise.

657. Telepathy is now a viable form of communication if you can afford it. For the very rich, tapping into the minds of anyone can happen with a click of a button. How does this discrepancy change social interactions?

658. Lasers have now replaced all guns. What makes this weapon so desirable is that it can shoot an unlimited number of bullets and is silent, making it an ideal tool amongst criminals. Your character is a member of the police force that must deal with this undetectable weapon.

659. Transportation is now more diverse than ever. For local travel you can choose from the following: bus, airbus, car, aircar, teleportation hub, bike, and of course, walking. How might your character commute to and from work?

660. Your character grew up thinking they were adopted. However, that couldn't be further from the truth. They are a clone. Created only to serve one singular purpose - be a walking organ donation site.

661. More advanced Artificial Intelligence is here. The technology is used for *everything*, from coming up with a bestselling novel to ensuring productivity on an assembly line. It's now hard to understand who is real and who isn't.

662. Many believe that time travel might one day be possible. Suppose that your character is the first one to discover how to travel through time. Where is the first place they go? What difficulties do they have when they get there?

663. Your character has just stumbled across a rare mineral that has never before been discovered. They learn that when this item is heated, it gives an unlimited amount of energy. However, upon cooling, it absorbs the amount equal to what was used. How do they make use of this strange tool?

664. Many works dealing with the future often focus on new technologies, social problems, and so forth. What about cities? What will be different about the way we live and work? Craft a scenario that deals with this.

665. Media has become a large part of our daily lives, from the ads shown continuously on our phones to the chosen media we view, like video games, TV, and films. In this narrative, your character must deal with a new form of media. What is it? How is your character involved in its creation?

666. What will humans look like in the future? Some theories suggest more enormous eyes and heads because of our dependency on the internet; while others believe we will become taller, with fewer organs. What do you think? Craft a scenario that features humans from the future.

667. Your character is one of the first people to test out a new piece of wearable transportation technology - a jetpack. They can choose to explore some new part of the world or use it for selfish gain. What do they do?

668. War has broken out, and if negotiations do not take place soon, billions will die. It isn't two cities or even countries at war, but two colonies of a distant planet.

669. Your character notices strange things happening around their house. First, a few dishes go missing, then the lights go out, and finally, someone begins to type messages on the computer. It's the first contact with another world! Aliens are trying to get your character's attention.

670. Your character has a scientific breakthrough, discovering that humans did not always live on Earth. How did they make this discovery, and what does it mean for humanity?

671. The planet is dying. Thousands of species are lost, and humans might be next. Your character will prevent that from happening by manning the first exploration of a potentially hospitable planet. Let's hope all goes well!

672. Your character has realized that someone has been following them. After a heated confrontation, they find out why. This person is warning your character about another person who has been using their DNA without permission. What for and how will your character put a stop to this?

673. What is hot in the world of fashion comes and goes frequently. Often, old trends eventually make their way back around. Take one style from a previous decade and let it inspire the fashion of the future.

674. Dystopias are a popular choice among writers when thinking of the future. Some might even say we are living in a dystopia right now. Craft your spin on this subgenre of fiction. Try to minimize tropes while still getting your themes across.

675. What is your vision of a perfect world? No more fighting, hunger, or pain of any sort? Write a narrative about this utopia, but showcase what kind of problem might exist if *no* problems exist.

676. Finally, hoverboards are here. These trendy gadgets can hang up to six feet off the ground and inspire a new sport. Your character is in the final match, hands around the ball. Then their hoverboard malfunctions.

677. 01101000 01100101 01101100 01110000 00100000 01101101 01100101 00001101 00001010. Your character receives this same message. What does it mean? Furthermore, where did this message come from?

The Past

There have been many pivotal moments throughout

history, all of which have an impact on the future. You may be living through an unprecedented time yourself. In this section, we will draw inspiration from pieces of the past that require examination.

678. Choose one object from antiquity; be it a vase, weapon, or sculpture, and use it in a short story. You can look up the details of this item or choose to create an account in which you take even more creative liberty.

679. Your character is behind enemy lines. Most of their comrades have not made it, and the sound of gunshots and bombs are getting closer. Will your character fulfill their mission before it's too late?

680. The Great Depression was a time of horrible fear and disenfranchisement; however, this period also saw the rise of new technologies. In this scenario, a character not only survives this period but also creates a world-changing business capitalizing on one of these new inventions.

681. Choose a global pandemic, such as the Spanish Flu, the Bubonic Plague, and take one of the front line workers' perspective, whether they are a doctor or trying to help keep the peace.

682. Your character is an immigrant that is escaping a harrowing situation back home. Write in detail how they manage to escape, what might happen if they don't, what would be waiting for them when they make it to their destination.

683. Farms have been a pivotal part of human existence throughout history. Write about a homestead that is threatened by outsiders. Focus on the idea of growing food and sustenance one moment, then trying to take up arms the next.

684. What might life have been like before electricity? Write a story in which a character experiences daily life before this technology but then hears about something that is supposed to "revolutionize the way we live."

685. When you think of a royal ball, what do you think of? Often, we think of a heteronormative romance between a king and what-will-be the future princess. Turn this narrative on its head. Feature two women love interests, have the princess be trans, have war break out, have the royal ball be a cover for a political issue, etc.

686. Did you know that there are currently more than 500 federally recognized indigenous tribes? Explore one of these and write a narrative in which your character encounters one of these communities. The story is about this character learning about the tribe's rich history and culture.

687. It is a case of mistaken identity. Write a story in which your character is accused of a crime they did not commit. It is then that the character learns that they were adopted at birth and have a twin.

688. Are you familiar with the concept of manifest destiny? It is the idea that American expansion was justifiable under self-motivated ideals. Write a scenario in which a character deals with this concept, from the side that is in danger of having their land taken away.

689. Imagine that your character is a peasant under serfdom. There is talk of an uprising, but your character isn't sure they want any part of it. Until something tragic happens, then they will join the cause and lead the first assault.

690. Choose a cause that you are passionate about and research the various movements and critical moments—for instance, The Civil Rights movement. Write a fictional account of a witness of one of these historical events.

691. The internet has changed almost every aspect of life. However, not too long ago, the internet wasn't available in most homes. Write a story in which a character has access to the internet for the first time. What sites do they visit? How do they feel about this new access to the information found within the computer?

692. In the late 19th and early 20th century, Safaris were popular amongst European and North American sportspeople. Write a scenario from the perspective of a local who does not want their hamlet visited by these outsiders.

693. Your character has contracted a disease that is wiping out thousands of people in the local community alone. Very soon, they will help scientists discover a vaccine - as an unwilling guinea pig.

694. Decide whether your character will be a hunter or a gatherer. If you choose a hunter, write a story about attacking a group of gatherers. If you are a gatherer, write about this assault. You can also choose to write a story that shifts between the perspective of both groups.

695. Your character is one of the first artists in history. Write a scenario in which they create a cave painting that will end up lasting for centuries. Then, write from the perspective of the individual who will discover it.

696. Your character is a part of an arranged marriage that neither parties want to be a part of. They are going to do whatever it takes to convince their parents that this isn't right, and it will never work. Finally, their parents agree, but there's a strange twist. What is the twist? How does it affect the would-be couple?

697. *Viva la Revolucion*! Long Live the Revolution! Thousands litter the streets, calling for the blood of the elite. Your character quivers; they are the elite.

698. Take a religious text and choose one story that resonates with you. If you are not religious, then you can choose one that you are interested in researching. Write a fictionalized account of this scene from the perspective of a silent observer.

699. Choose one piece of technology from the last century and write a story in which an individual uses it for the first time. What problems do they have? Do they decide to give up this invention and go back to life without it?

700. *Mush!* One of the most famous sled dog stories is Balto, where this dog and its companions delivered medicine despite the bleak winter. Research a less known sled dog and write a story about its tale.

701. Craft a scenario in which your character is an astronaut who ends up not making it to space. What famous person goes instead? Why weren't they able to make it? How do they help support the space program instead?

702. A great famine has occurred throughout the land. Your character has been doing what they can to help the populace, but resources are still dwindling. One day your character pays an unexpected visit to the town's leader. There they discover that the leader has been stockpiling food while others starve.

703. Choose a pivotal moment in history and write a historical romance. However, have this romance be contrary to the expectations of the time. Keep in mind how power, who has it and who doesn't, affects your chosen couple.

704. The "Great Flood" is an event that occurs in many world religions. Write a scenario in which your character is one of the survivors of this flood. How do they move forward after so many of their friends and loved ones are lost?

705. Are you a pet lover? What is your favorite domesticated animal? In this scenario, write about the first person to own this creature. You could also be even more specific and choose a particular kind of breed.

706. Your character is a Roman soldier tasked with escorting a man named Julius Caesar to the senate chambers. You have heard murmurs that something terrible might happen there. Though, you aren't sure what....

707. Many different cultures have had a matriarchy throughout history. Research one and write a scenario in which your character is the next in line to be Queen. What anxieties and fears do they have? What might happen if another wants to challenge the throne?

708. I love castles, but I can't imagine living in one. So many rooms! Write a scene where a new member of a court, be it worker or royalty, gets lost. The more they try to find their way around, the further they get from their destination. It's almost as if the castle itself is alive.

709. Research the year you were born and find one event that interests you. Using this event, create a short story that showcases what you have learned.

710. What do you think the earliest conversation might have been? Perhaps it was two cave dwellers warning each other about a hungry beast. Maybe it was a confession of sorts. Write a dialogue-only story that explores this.

Finding Inspiration

When someone asks me where an idea for a short story comes from, I usually say, "Everywhere." A good idea doesn't just come from one source but many different places. Your brain makes connections, and a story comes out. This section will give you plenty of references to draw from.

711. Think of three songs; the first song should be one that you loved as a child, the second as a teen, and the third you currently love. Combine all of these into a short story.

712. The news can be a good source of information, whether we use it to inspire us from a feel-good piece or use the news to analyze some part of the human condition we do not understand. Choose one of these to write about.

713. Letters may seem like a thing of the past, but we can use them to create new and modern works. Use a previous message you have written and use some element in a scene. If you do not have an old letter, write a new letter to someone you care about, and use this instead.

714. Go to the library and choose three books at random. Find a character from the first book and write down a list of attributes you like. From the second book, choose one location and write down a similar place it reminds you of. From the final book, write down three problems the protagonists face. Use all of these to create a new story.

715. One of the best things you can do to help your writing is to take a break from it! Take a long walk, whether it is around the neighborhood or a hiking trail. Let your mind wander. By the end of it, incorporate some of these thoughts into a new story entirely.

716. Find a piece of your old writing, from a previous manuscript to something you did for school or work. You have two choices - either revise it or let it inspire you to create something new.

717. Nature is an excellent well of inspiration. Find a spot where you can get lost in a natural environment. It can be a lake, river, trail, mountain, etc. Write a 300-word description of the location you have chosen. Use this as a future setting.

718. What is your best memory? The most painful? Take elements from the worst and best to create a scenario in which a character deals with both.

719. Use a dictionary, whether online or with a physical book, to gather a list of 10 words at random. What connections can you make between these words? Draw from these to create a short story.

720. Recruit your family or friends. Ask at least five individuals to give you a plot idea. You can have these ideas in your arsenal for later works, or you can combine them into something new. Remember, give credit where credit is due!

721. For the next few days, write down any significant dreams that you can remember. Are there any symbols or scenarios that repeat themselves? Explore this through your writing.

722. One of my sources of inspiration is through my pets. Not only have I included them in various characters, but they tend to get into all sorts of mischief. Use your pets, or someone else's, as a catalyst for a scene.

723. What are your primary life goals aside from writing? Take one of these goals and incorporate them into a short story. Have a character spend their time trying to accomplish the same thing.

724. What is your favorite color? Research some trivia about this color and use this to craft a new story. For instance, did you know that the red stripes on the United States flag stand for courage? From this, you could come up with a tale featuring a soldier in battle.

725. Choose a spot where you can be a silent people observer, such as a cafe or bookstore. Write down any snippets of dialogue you overhear and incorporate this into a scene.

726. Find an article or blog about a topic you are interested in. Using this as a springboard, create a scene that uses only this research. Once finished, research the matter further and see if any discrepancy might arise.

727. Are you a huge film fan? Whether you prefer books or movies, write down a list of your top 10 films of all time. Is there any unifying theme between them all? Use these themes to come up with a fresh new story of your own.

728. I'm a sucker for a good quote. I am continually sharing them with others or using them to motivate myself. Find quotes that resonate with you. In what ways do these inspire your writing?

729. Change up your writing process and do the opposite of what works typically. If you write in the morning, write at night. If you write after a good workout, write before. How does your writing differ? Do new elements emerge in your story?

730. Good smells. Bad smells. Sometimes hard-to-discern smells. Write a story in which aromas feature a prominent role. Only include smells you have personally smelt, and thus, could write an adequate description on.

731. Write down two columns, the first containing 20 likes you have, and the second 20 dislikes. These can be as simple or complex as you prefer. Mix and match some of these to incorporate into various subplots.

732. Too often, we throw away ideas never to reuse them. This time, every time you have an idea, you don't think will work, write it down as part of an "inspiration bank." Each time you need to inspire yourself, return to this list of once discarded ideas.

733. Where would your dream vacation be? What about your favorite place to visit? Write a story that incorporates both of these. Try to make it somewhere that your character is not too familiar with for added tension.

734. Themes are an essential part of any great novel. Create a story centered on one of these themes: unrequited love, good versus evil, overcoming prejudice, coming of age, deception, or the circle of life.

735. Declutter your space! Whether it is your desk or your whole house, decluttering can be extremely therapeutic. When you begin to declutter, you may find items that inspire you to create throughout the process.

736. As shown in the previous category, objects from our history can be incredibly inspiring. Now, choose a moment from your life and let that inspire you directly. For instance, you can write about the first time you lost a pet, or the first time you fell in love, and so on.

737. Do you have a best friend? Maybe when you were younger? Think of the closest friend you've ever had and think of some secret you told them or wish you told them. Use a similar scene in a larger story.

738. Ask someone what questions they had about life when they were a child. For instance, *why is the sky* *blue?* Or perhaps, *why do we need money?* Use one of these questions and turn it into a folktale in which you explain the answer.

739. Do you belong to any writing forums? What about a writing-oriented social media group? These are often places where we can leverage others to help work through story problems. Offer up one plot idea and then ask others to help you build upon it.

740. Even if you are not an artist, spend some time creating artwork. Do not tie this piece to any of your current manuscripts. What did you end up drawing? Use this to create a brand new story entirely.

741. Choose three completely unrelated magazines, for instance, a motorcycle magazine and a beauty magazine. Use some of the subtopics within these magazines and create three intertwined scenes.

742. Write down a list of 10 adjectives, 10 adverbs, and 10 nouns. Use these as a word bank to inspire you whenever you hit a wall with your writing.

Characters of All Sorts

While the previous section focuses on more of an interior look at how a character feels, these prompts focus on who they *are*—occupations, what type of personality traits they have, their motivations, etc.

Personality Traits

How might someone describe your character? What would your character say their best personality trait is? Some of us have a reputation for being sweet and kind, while others have a reputation for being rude and pretentious. No matter where your character falls, these prompts deal with all kinds of personality types.

743. Your character is exceptionally messy. Ever since they have moved out of their parents' house, that trait has only increased. Soon their small, one-bedroom apartment is filled with clothes, leftover food wrappers, and general trash. Are they still just a messy person, or is this a sign of a larger issue?

744. Your character is a sucker for hiking, rowing, mountain climbing, and anything that fulfills their adventurous nature. This time they find a challenge that will be sure to give them the thrill of their life. What is it, and more importantly, will they survive?

745. No matter who your character is speaking to, they always feel an air of superiority. They don't have any particular reason why they should showcase such arrogance, but that's okay. They will soon find themselves down on their luck, with no one to turn to since they have pushed everyone away.

746. It doesn't matter what their friends and family say; your character refuses to believe they are raising a spoiled child. Sure, they give their child everything they want, but where is the harm in that? Aside from the temper tantrums, of course.

747. Your character spends much of their time in the office, always working on one more deal. They have no time for friends, family, and especially not any time for themselves. One day they finally make it home to see all of their loved ones have staged an intervention over their workaholic nature.

748. No one trusts your character. They are incredibly dishonest about all matters in their life, from telling little white lies to outright bending the truth. One day they tell a lie to precisely the wrong person.

749. Your character has accomplished a great deal in their life. They got a Bachelor's at 16, a Master's at 19, a Ph.D. by 26, and a full-time job as the department head at the top research company at 29. However, by 35, they have reached significant burnout, tired of the need to be smart all the time.

750. "Are you done yet? It's been 20 minutes!" Your character is known far and wide for their impatience. While most everyone else believes they are simply rude, there is a reason for their inability to wait. What is it?

751. Your character can't seem to sit still. One minute they will be having a casual conversation, and the next, they are running away for an adventure. This restlessness and impulsivity will soon put them in harm's way.

752. Like most teens, your character has a touch of apathy. They don't seem to care about their family, their used-to-be favorite hobbies, and especially not school. All of that is going to change when they discover a newfound passion. This is a hobby that no one else saw coming. What is it?

753. Not even their closest family members know what your character is hiding. They come into the house, mumble quick hellos, and then head down into the basement before coming back up and pretending nothing is wrong. If another character might chance down there, what would they find?

754. There's not much to say about your character other than the fact that they are rude. No matter who they are speaking to, they interrupt the other person, make snide remarks, and generally give everyone around them a hard time. Suppose this rudeness stems from a traumatic experience in their past. Can your character come to terms with what happened and find a way to grow as a person?

755. "Grow up" is something that your character hears often. Ever the practical joker, your character has certainly been accused of being too silly or having their head in the clouds. Your character says that they have a zest for life, but is this truly the reason why they never take anything seriously?

756. Your character has an innate musical gift, from singing to playing any instrument they touch. They take each compliment with grace and have never pursued anything creatively. However, that is about to change when someone they care about convinces them to go after their dreams.

757. Your character is incredibly nurturing. They have rescued baby birds, looked after children, and genuinely cared for anyone who comes across their past. After getting into a terrible accident, it is time for them to get nurtured back to health. Who is the one that will come to their aid?

758. No matter what obstacle is in front of them, your character has an air of determination. They will see each task through, even at the risk of their sanity. Then one day, they come across a downright impossible feat. No one has ever accomplished this before. What is it? Can their willpower remain?

759. Your character lives under a cloud of constant praise. Even if they make a mistake, their parents are quick to only focus on the positive. This causes your character to develop a false sense of talent and ability, which will affect them later in life when they have to take criticism as part of their job.

760. Your character could undoubtedly be considered brave. They have bested a bear while hiking in the mountains, survived a fiery plane crash, and even rescued a swimmer from a hungry shark. Your character would disagree with the idea that they are courageous, however. Instead, they feel that they are just unlucky.

761. Your character is pretty open-minded and will try anything once. Trying new foods, new styles of clothes, new relationships; your character is open to anything. Now they are met with a situation they are not so sure about. Why the hesitation?

762. If there is a job to be done, your character is happy to help do it. Although just a child, they are eager to attend to the needs of everyone around them. Their helpful nature is starting to take a toll on their young life, however. What will be the breaking point?

763. For many years, your character thought they were just shy. They didn't like crowds, they didn't make eye contact, and they certainly avoided phone calls like the plague. Then, later in life, they finally get a diagnosis and can finally breathe a little easier. What is the diagnosis, and how does having it help them?

764. Thus far, your character has been tricked into eating a bug, gone to work wearing a banana costume, and drove 40 miles to see a dragon that didn't exist. Calling them gullible would be an understatement. Create a funny story featuring this overtly trustful character.

765. *Take, take, take* – that's all your character ever does. "Sharing is caring" is a phrase they like to use, but this only seems to apply to others. Finally, all their friends and loved ones have had enough and are determined to teach them a lesson.

766. Your character often rejects the help of others. They have lived alone since they were 18 and are happy to live entirely on their own until they die. They've even downright refused help when offered to them. Then something happens that forces them to reach out.

767. Your character is obsessed with the very idea of love. They have been married three times and have had countless dates that went nowhere. Your character tells themselves that they are unloveable, but their clinginess and fear of rejection are pushing everyone away in reality.

768. After being out of work for seven months, your character is at their wit's end. They have applied for over 100 different jobs, went on several job fairs, and even did an unpaid internship hoping it would lead to a new position. Then they get a job affair – as the next grim reaper.

769. Suppose your character has the opposite problem: they have a job they hate but have never left because of the security it provides. Now that they have saved up enough to start a new business venture, they are going to quit – in the most dramatic way possible.

770. Despite the best efforts of law enforcement and volunteers, a missing child remains unfound. That child is your character, who is now grown up. They have an inkling that something about their life isn't right and are about to find out their true story. Focus primarily on how they get back to their old family and what kind of trauma and personality they develop due to their abduction.

771. Your character is the CEO of a major player in the technology industry. They are known for being belligerent, demanding, and rude. Write a story in which this character ends up working for the lowest level employee. How does that happen? Do they have a change of heart?

772. Your character, currently the most famous artist globally, is scheduled for a new gallery opening in a week. They are supposed to release new work, but there is a problem. The person they have been paying to do the actual artwork suddenly quits. Your character cannot even draw a stick figure. What are they going to do?

773. Your character's love interest is frugal to the point where they will use the same water for bathing, doing laundry, and flushing the toilet. On more than one occasion, your character has asked to borrow money, and their partner won't even spare one cent. Your character has tried to be understanding, assuming their love is going through tough times. Then they find out a little secret – their significant other is worth millions.

774. Everyone loves your character because they are so sweet. No matter what someone does to them, your character always responds with a forgiving nature and can-do attitude. All of this is just a façade, of course, for a darker secret.

775. Someone's angel is someone else's devil. Use this in literal terms for a short story. Suppose your character is a double agent, working on the side of heaven as well as hell. Will they get caught by either side?

Protagonists

The protagonist is often called the hero of the story, but that's not always the case. The protagonist is simply the main character, the one who guides the plot along. They can be morally ambiguous, even make decisions that contradict what the readers would likely choose. The key is to create a character that the audience can follow through the arc of the story.

776. Your character is an older superhero who has spent their entire life-saving others. They've also reaped the benefits – from being on movie posters to a whole line of action figures created in their likeness. At their retirement party, a close friend reveals a secret that may change public perception.

777. Your character is part of a sports team that has the least likely shot of winning. Somehow they win a big game. Then another, and another! Are they cheating somehow, or is this a classic tale of the underdogs finally getting their day in the sun?

778. From somewhere underneath the house, your character hears small whimpers. They make their way, belly against the ground, into the crawlspace to discover puppies. Your character spends the next few weeks nursing these babies back to health, all while hoping their parents don't find out.

779. Your character is a single parent who has been struggling to make ends meet. While checking the mail one day, they are shocked to see someone has sent an anonymous check for a million dollars. However, it comes with a price.

780. The thought of the child's death has never left your character's mind. As a lifeguard, they feel the burden squarely on their shoulders. Now they have a chance to make things right for the grieving family. But how?

781. Your character is the newest child at a small-town elementary school, where everyone knows everyone. Their first day is rough, and the second day is even worse. Your character can use their powers to ward off the bullies, but doing so might make them move again.

782. Write a short story about a character who is the first of their kind in a high ranking position. They could be the first female president, the first king from another world, etc.

783. Your character is a full-time college student, a full-time employee, a volunteer, and an RA. Now they have been asked to help out a friend who is in desperate need. How does your character manage this extra burden?

784. Your character has been judged by others most of their adult life. They have struggled with addiction for years. Now, they are trying to get themselves clean, but rehab turns out to be much more challenging than they anticipated. Write an inspiring tale about this character's struggles and hardships, focusing on the trauma and social reasons associated with drug addiction.

785. After a colossal hurricane almost decimates a small island, your character signs up to render first response aid. When they get there, they realize that another unexpected storm is coming. This one will be much worse than the first.

786. Your character is a firefighter transporting a family from their house to the safety zone. The winds suddenly change. The fire is now headed straight for your character and this small group. They will have to decide whether to seek shelter or try to outrun nature.

787. Are protestors ever seen as the "good guys?" Certainly not by the ones that they are protesting. Shake that up! Write a story in which a group of protestors saves the lives of the people they are advocating against. You could also write the reverse.

788. The world looks different when you are by yourself, alone in the woods, 40 miles from civilization. Of course, your character didn't choose to end up here. Somehow they have gotten off trail and are struggling to survive as they try to make their way back home.

789. Well into their eighties, your character has had a lifetime of regrets, from the business they didn't start to the relationships they never had. When they are diagnosed with a terminal illness, your character decides to live their life to the fullest. Where do they start?

790. They may be adorable, but they still have a job to do. In this scenario, take a service dog's perspective as they go about their daily routine.

791. Your character is quarantined, much like the entire world, due to an uncontrollable virus. Your character does not have the virus, but someone very close to them does. They must take care of this person and deal with limited resources, all while trying to keep themselves from getting sick.

792. After a lifetime in the STEM field, your character decides it's time to retire. They decide to take up painting and realize that they have a natural talent for it. Very soon, your character's art is in demand the world over. Is it time to pick up a new career? Or stop before the pressure grows too high?

793. It's been almost three days since your character last had food. Water is also running low. Your character always thought that, if their plane crash-landed on a deserted island, they would know what to do. This isn't the case at all!

794. After almost a decade of hard work, your character has saved up enough to have their own small business. What is it, and what could go wrong during the grand opening?

795. Your character has always dreamed of being a bestselling author. However, after almost 3,000 rejections, they have decided to give up on traditional publishing. They self publish their first book, and it becomes an overnight success. How do they handle their newfound fortune and the criticisms that come along with publishing this route?

796. It's the annual family vacation, but something goes wrong. Your young character must take care of the rest of their family after becoming lost in a foreign country.

797. There have been many stories about characters who strive to complete a bucket list, usually older or those with terminal illnesses. Write a story in which a young, healthy person decides to help someone else with their bucket list, risking their own lives in the process.

798. Your character has been with the detective agency for over twenty years. However, soon they get a case that would make even the most hardboiled investigator question humanity.

799. Biological and adoptive parents often get lots of love. What about foster parents? Write a short story in which a foster parent changes the life of many different children. When the foster parent has hardships later in life, these now-grown children show up to help them out.

800. Your character is one of the most trusted babysitters on the block. This is put to the test when an intruder breaks in. How does their wit match up against an individual intent on harming the children?

801. The ones that earn the most respect at an organization are usually those at the top—the CEOs, COOs, CFOs, etc. However, your character, a recently hired intern, is about to make their appearance known in a big way.

802. Write a story in which a soldier meets and falls in love with someone from the other side, but find a way to break this familiar trope. For instance, the other person does not love the soldier, but the soldier helps them anyway.

803. Your character has just donated a kidney. Naturally, this is typically considered a brave and heroic act. However, there is one problem – your character did not agree to this.

804. Twin hurricanes hit a small coastal city, leaving 5ft of standing water in its wake. Resources are low, and violence begins to erupt. Write from the perspective of one of these storm survivors.

805. Your character works at a nursing home. Typically, each day is tiresome, but it is relatively standard. Then one day, a patient comes in, old and feeble. The next day, they look a little bit healthier. The next day, they are not only healthier but also younger. It seems they are aging in reverse.

806. In just the past month, your character has been a clown, superhero, lovable dinosaur, and magician. What job allows them to tackle all of these unique roles? They are an entertainer for a children's hospital.

807. Usually, a knight must protect a kingdom from a dragon. This time, spin a tale in which a dragon must defend the domain from a group of rogue knights.

808. Your character is on the front line of a war, but it isn't against a country. It's against a global pandemic. Your character is in the epicenter, working with an elite team of doctors to locate patient zero and find a cure before it's too late.

809. Your character is a judge who is considered tough on crime. Very rarely do they dismiss cases. However, this particular case not only tugs at their heartstrings but causes them to question the judicial system itself.

810. Sometimes the best protagonists are those who do incredible things under ordinary circumstances. Write a short story in which an average person does something extraordinary.

Antagonists

For every hero, there is a villain. At least, that is the label that antagonists often get. However, it is crucial to keep in mind that even characters with the worst intention should not believe what they are doing is wrong. The best antagonists have a clear cut motivation for the evil deeds they commit.

811. Your character stands over their now-living creation and screams, "It's Alive! Alive!" The humanoid figure is very much alive, but will it be as loyal and subservient as the professor hopes? Craft a new take on the classic story of *Frankenstein*.

812. Mussolini, Hitler, Hussein – these are infamous leaders who disregarded human life for their own selfish goals. Your character works for a notorious dictator whether they have done so by force or by choice. What lessons can this narrative bring to the reader?

813. Your character is one of the most successful computer hackers in the entire world. A secret organization recruits them to break into one of the most heavily guarded computer networks. But why?

814. Your character sits behind bars, accused of being a war criminal. They claim that the government has the wrong person. It wasn't them, and this is all a case of mistaken identity. Is that true? Or, is your character just trying to cover up for their terrible crimes?

815. "Follow me, and you shall be rewarded seven-fold." Your character stands before thousands of onlookers; all convinced that your character is a living deity. Your character didn't intend on being a cult leader. Not really. Write a story that explains how your character amassed their following. More importantly, give insight into whether or not they will continue this facade.

816. Your character is a part of a small hamlet in which terrible occurrences begin to happen. First, a group of chickens goes missing, then a whole cow, and finally, a farmer is found mauled to death. Your character doesn't want to be the cause of all this, but being a werewolf, these evil deeds are kind of inevitable.

817. "Hey, stop you!" Your character takes off running, pushing past people in a crowded city. They clutch the purse tighter underneath a tucked arm. Your character fears dropping their bounty, but they fear getting caught even more. Why have they decided to steal in the first place?

818. Your character lets out a long sigh, staring through the car window at their next target. On the seat next to them, a loaded gun lies in wait. Your character is a contract killer who is tired of the life they live. Will this be their last job?

819. Sailing the seven seas and collecting treasure isn't all it's cracked up to be. Your character is one of the most infamous pirates of all time, an actual conquer of the ocean. However, it is the land they are now after. Is it because of a person or merely looking for a different type of adventure?

820. There has already been a book about a serial killer that kills serial killers, serial killers that help police catch other killers, and all manners of evil serial killers that are just the regular kind of evil. This time take the perspective of a victim who got away and their journey to bring down the person who almost murdered them.

821. Crime doesn't pay, but your character has made loads of money. They have sold drugs, burglarized houses, and committed acts of petty theft. Now, they are going to go after their most significant criminal act yet. What is it? Will karma, and the law, finally catch up to them?

822. In another crime scenario, suppose your character is a mob boss with thousands of people working underneath them. One day one of the lowest underlinings ends up murdered. No big deal; it happens all the time. Then two more underlings. Then a street boss, then that person's boss. It seems a vengeful killer is working up the mafia ladder – to get to your character!

823. The "Evil StepMother" is such a common trope when it comes to princes and princesses. Turn this trope entirely on its head. Write from the perspective of a stepmother deemed evil by everyone around her, but honestly, they are doing what's best for their stepchild.

824. Your character is the CEO of a large company. They are one of those who believe that the sun rises and sets on them, unaware of how others feel. They also don't realize that all of the subordinates have been planning out their revenge for months. The day has finally come for the work community to teach your character a lesson.

825. "Someone has poisoned our King!" The gathered guards immediately arrest the person who handed the King their nightly goblet of wine - your character. Are they truly responsible for killing the kingdom's beloved leader, or is your character innocent?

826. Your character stands in the shadows of a home that is not theirs. They were worried the alarm might have gone off, but the only sound was their staggered breathing. What are they doing here? What will happen when the homeowner inevitably finds out?

827. The movies might make carjacking look so cool, but real life is far more complex. Write a more realistic portrayal of a group of thieves. Are they stealing out of financial necessity or for the thrill of the ride?

828. Your character is torn. On the one hand, they could gain three million dollars. On the other hand, the child they have kidnapped for ransom starts to tug on their heartstrings. What's it going to be? Money or morality?

829. Is your character the evil twin? Write a scenario in which your character is the one who commits misdeeds or the one who keeps getting blamed for them. If your character is "bad," what makes them this way?

830. Your character has created a robot that will only do their bidding. At first, they only make this robot clean up after them, water the plants when they are not home, and pick the occasional pocket, but then the tasks become more serious. Write an escalation piece in which the robot begins to commit more dangerous acts for its owner.

831. Your character must make a decision, and they have precisely one minute to do it. They are a spy who has been caught by the enemy. Behind their ear is a poisonous capsule. Will your character secretly take it, accept the torture, but never talk, or will they sing like a bird?

832. Your character is a pilot who is about to drop a bomb on a major city. Will they do so, or will they decide to disobey orders? Write a story that begins with them entering the jet, takeoff, the flight itself, and have the story end at that final decision.

833. Your character has finally lit their last match. As a known arsonist, they have been wanted by the police for a long time. What excuses do they have for causing so much trouble for so many? Were any lives lost in these blazes, or did your character target vacant houses? Does this change things morally if they did?

834. Almost everyone that does any sort of online financial transactions has had their information stolen. Credit card and banking fraud is a nightmare to deal with. Write a scene in which your character is one of these identity thieves. How did they get into this "profession," and will they ever stop?

835. It is the Wild West, and your character is a known bandit. They are about to pull off their biggest heist yet, but with their face on every wanted poster in the town, are they going to pull this off?

836. Your character is a schoolyard bully responsible for many bruises and tears. When a new kid moves to town, your character starts to have a change of heart. How does this new student influence your character's sudden anti-bullying stance?

837. Someone has been stealing items out of college dorms. First, it's an extra pair of headphones and the occasional bag of snacks. Then it's laptops and smartphones. All fingers point to your character, the only RA who has access to the master key. Write a story in which your character showcases their innocence or one in which they finally come clean?

838. *Just put one foot in front of the other. Don't let them know you are following them.* Your character is a stalker, who often has an inner monologue with themselves. Delve into this person's head in a bid to find out what went so wrong.

839. Choose to write from the perspective of one of the following: a rude waiter who purposely puts unspeakable things in guests' food or a patron who is incredibly pretentious and loves giving staff members a hard time. Write a scene in which these two interact.

840. Write from the perspective of one of the most loathed figures in the city – the parking attendant, ever getting yelled at by frustrated car owners when your character is just doing their job.

841. Three lungs. Two livers. A Heart. A couple of eyes. It's a great day for a body snatcher. That is until they suddenly are on the receiving end of someone seeking revenge.

842. Your character is the person that everyone at the bar hates – the one that hits on everyone and then gets obnoxious and rude when rejected. Then, they aggressively flirt with someone who will teach them a lesson they'll never forget.

Occupations

Some jobs can be stressful. Some can be enjoyable. Some jobs can be inspiring, while others can lead you to make career changes or direct you to an even better position. No matter what, jobs can also be immensely entertaining.

843. Your character's first job is as a camp counselor. They do arts and crafts with the students, teach them about nature, and take them on small hikes. Today is a hiking day, and by the end of it, your character realizes that one of the kids is missing.

844. Your character is a sculptor that primarily creates inanimate objects, animals, and strange creatures. On a whim, they decide to sculpt a human figure, only to have the model come to life. Their creation enthralls the artist until they realize, as they look at a nearby chimera, stag, and oversized scorpion, that if this figure has come to life - perhaps something else might too.

845. It has been years since your character was a personal trainer to the stars. They've let themselves go, have stopped engaging in any fitness activity - all because of some tabloids about them and an A list celebrity who became a D-lister after a few "training sessions." Now, that celebrity is going to make a comeback, and they've asked for your character's help to do it.

846. Your character is a private investigator currently at a stakeout. After a long night, with very little sleep, they intend to close their eyes only for a minute or so. A few minutes turns into half an hour, and then an hour. They awake to the sound of someone knocking on their car window. It's the target!

847. Your character lives on a famous island destination and works as a tour guide. While they are pointing out some local history to guests, a deep rumbling is heard, followed by a small Earthquake. The volcano right next to the group is about to explode.

848. Nothing ever seems to happen at your character's place of work. Customers come in, buy chips, cookies, and other snacks in addition to gas, and only occasionally is there an issue with the gas pumps themselves. Then one day, while your character is at the register, someone walks in that will change their life forever.

849. Your character is an intern at a large multinational corporation. Typically, their day consists of running errands for the higher-ups under the guise of "learning to multitask" while getting yelled at by the

CEO because of reasons your character has no control over. One day, your character decides they've had enough. They recruit the help of other subordinates to get their revenge.

850. Your character hears both cheers and jeers from the audience that gathers on the corner. As a street performer, they know some people like them, and some don't. What they aren't expecting is for someone to drop a million dollar check in the tip jar. Is this real? Or, is this a practical joke from an annoyed onlooker?

851. Working in a library is an excellent job for any certified bibliophile. Your character feels as though they have won the job lottery. Not only do they have access to books day in and day out, but they can share that love of reading with others. However, when the library's funding gets cut, it is now up to your character to save the day.

852. "We need more daisies!" "Not everyone likes red velvet!" "Sorry, but my cousin Jake can't sit near his cousin James!" Your character hears all kinds of requests from their clients. However, as a wedding planner, it is your character's job to make magic happen. Then an odd request comes in. The couple doesn't want a wedding planned for them, but rather their dogs.

853. During the early days of the telephone, switchboard operators directed calls. Research this outdated profession and create a story from the perspective of someone recently hired for the role. How did they deal with this developing technology, and what strange calls did they receive?

854. While being a stage performer might not seem like a stressful job, it can often be, especially on opening nights. Tonight is one such performance. Your character is an understudy. Right before the curtain goes up, the lead performer has a fatal heart attack. It's up to your character to single-handedly prove that the show can go on.

855. Your character is performing open-heart surgery on a patient when they find a strange anomaly. The patient's heart isn't a heart at all! What is it? And how is the patient still alive?

856. Your character has groomed many different breeds of dogs, from chihuahuas to Great Danes. They've even groomed a cat or two. However, this time someone comes in with a lion!

857. Being an electrician is hard work, primarily because of the danger involved. Your character gets called out to a house to reinstall some new lights in the basement. When the lights go on, your character cries out in horror. The new light illuminates something the homeowner thought they could keep hidden. What is it?

858. Your character is known as "The Shark," aka one of the harshest criminal prosecutors around. They have probably put hundreds of people behind bars. This time a case comes in that makes them question everything they knew about criminal law. They are sure the person is innocent, but it isn't up to them to prove it, and doing so just might cost them their career.

859. Your character is a freelance graphic designer that often gets offers of "experience" instead of pay. Normally, they ignore such requests and focus on real work, but today they've had enough. Write a story about a graphic designer who gets revenge on those looking to get the job done for free.

860. "Open wide!" Your character, a dentist, leans into the mouth of the patient and oddly gasps. It's common to see patients with long canines, who choose to alter their teeth somehow, but this patient has FANGS. Long ones. And x-rays don't lie. Are they dealing with a real vampire?

861. Ever since horror movies started with the killer clown trope, your character has trouble working as a party entertainer. Making kids smile is their passion, but most kids run and scream. Your character decides that if it's a killer clown these people want, it's what they will get - starting with the horror community.

862. With climate change affecting the growing seasons, your character, a farmer, produces fewer crops each year. While picking up seeds at a local feed store, they find a package with no label. The seller has no idea where they came from but sells them to your character anyway. When planted, your character discovers that this strange crop is the key to solving world hunger.

863. Your character is a delivery driver for a bustling restaurant. During a rush order, your character goes way above the speed limit and crashes. The car skids off the highway, into a collection of trees, and too far for any passerby to see. Shaken but not injured, your character must survive using only the food that caused them to speed in the first place.

864. The phones have been ringing all day, and your character is at their wit's end. They've been a receptionist at the company for years, and they've never had this many calls before. Each ring is from an entirely different person, and each caller is angrier than the last. What prompted this frustration from the masses?

865. Your character is finally going to see their dream realized. They are going to open their company's doors for the first time. As a new startup, there's a lot that can go wrong. Write a scenario that walks readers through the first day of the CEO's new venture.

866. Your character is a bartender at one of the hottest nightclubs in town. Usually, they spend most of their evening mixing drinks, but this time they spend most of their evening chatting up a new patron. Your character is so smitten that they fail to realize that this customer is no ordinary guest. Who is this attractive customer, and are they equally interested in your character?

867. Selling houses is what your character excels the most at. As a real estate agent, they have sold mansions, cottages, and everything in between. They have also worked for several different clients, from small families to CEOs. This time, they are working for the undead, who want their home sold to someone willing to share the property.

868. With each passing generation, your character is becoming more and more disenfranchised. Being a high school teacher is hard enough, but being one where the kids all have access to social media and care about little else, is downright frustrating. This time your character creates an inventive way to get their students motivated about learning. It's too bad the school board wants them to stop immediately.

869. Your character knows nine different languages and is a top-ranking translator at a secret government facility. One day they receive a particular assignment where they have to learn an alien species' language.

870. Your character is trapped in the middle of a war-torn city, armed with only a camera. They have taken enough pictures to prove that what they are reporting is real, but now they need to make it out of the city alive.

871. For the past 40 years, your character has hosted a popular game show. It is their last show, and they fully intend to retire. However, not only are they the only one who knows this fact, but your character plans to choose someone in the audience to be the next host – whether they want to or not.

872. "Is my dinner ready yet?" "Are my socks clean?" "Aren't you done yet!?" When your character signed up to be a wealthy family's assistant, they didn't realize they would also be a butler, maid, dog walker, accountant, chef, nutritionist, and so on. The pay is good, but not the attitude. Your character vows to get revenge on this entitled, self-absorbed family, but how?

873. Your character is a digital marketer for a large publishing house. They have just been assigned a new book to market and, during the research process, find out the book is plagiarized. Do they alert the publishing house or try to keep things quiet?

874. While most people believe fishing is a leisurely activity, your character knows that being a professional angler takes hard work and dedication. Especially when they are looking to beat a world record, if all goes well, they will get the notoriety they are after. If it goes poorly, they might lose more than just the big fish.

Sports, Animals, & Misc.

Although we often look at the most significant moments of our lives (from weddings to funerals), our existence contains many smaller, day-to-day moments. This section will pay close attention to everything that makes us human, from the games we loved to play as a child to the pets we used to have, and everything in between.

Playing Games

From birth until death, one of the best ways to connect with others is by playing games. We play games out of boredom, for fellowship, and sometimes, we do it to assert our power over others. Games make their appearance in many different facets of our life.

875. Your young character is playing a rousing game of hide-n-seek with their older siblings. They find a great hiding place that works just a little too well. It's been a whole hour, and they still haven't been found yet. Have they been forgotten about?

876. Tag is one of the most popular children's games of all time. There's something just so magical about chasing your friends, tagging them, and then giving them the gift of being "It." However, your character decides to put a new spin on this old classic. What is it?

877. Your character *loathes* gym class. It isn't so much as the physicality required, but more so that each class ends with a giant dodgeball session, and your character seems to be the primary target.

878. It's a board game night! Each Friday, your character and their friends play a brand new roleplaying game. However, this night something has changed. The game is about to get real - literally.

879. Heads Up, 7-Up is a game that teachers love as it requires total silence. To participate, students must put their heads on their desks and put one of their thumbs-up. The small group of leaders must then touch some of their classmates. When time is up, the students must guess who has tagged them. This game is about to get a little strange when someone claims a ghost has touched their thumb. Is the student telling a lie, or is there a spirit in the classroom?

880. It is a game that has frustrated many players, even causing large fights between family members. This time your character is playing a life-or-death version of the world's most popular board game. Now, buying up all the railroads and the expensive property is the key to staying alive.

881. Your character takes a deep breath, hands trembling against the cold steel. They pull the trigger and audibly let out a sigh of relief before passing the gun to the next person. They didn't choose to play this game of Russian Roulette; they were forced.

882. "Got any 10s?" Your character's opponent shakes their head. "Go Fish." While this is usually considered a kid's game, these adults play it for the millions of dollars at stake.

883. Suppose that your character is playing high stakes poker and has won almost every hand dealt. That's because they are cheating and are about to be caught.

884. During some family downtime, your character joins in on a game of dominos. Several rounds later, tensions begin to rise, and soon the police are called. How did this family-friendly game escalate so quickly?

885. At the fair, your character has been winning every single carnival game they play to the point that security guards want to question them about their alleged cheating. The funny thing is, they aren't cheating at all. Your character is just that good.

886. It doesn't matter what game someone plays on their smartphone; it can be extremely addictive. This is what happens to your character. They can't stop playing! In a bid to free themselves from this gaming addiction, they decide to target the makers of the app themselves.

887. Your character has lived in the neighborhood their whole life. In their old age, they have become somewhat cruel and are prone to yelling at people, especially children, to keep quiet. All of that is going to change when they see a few children playing jump rope. What is it about this game that will change their heart for the better?

888. Your character is in the middle of a rousing game of chicken, though instead of a car, they are squarely on someone else's shoulders in the pool. They give their opponent one hard push, and then the unthinkable happens. The other player doesn't fall back into the water but hits their head on the concrete siding.

889. Your character has spent countless hours playing 90s Windows Solitaire. More so than perhaps even the creator himself. While playing their usual nightly game, your character notices something they have never spotted before—a hidden message.

890. Your character holds the highest score on the most popular game in the Arcade. There's no way anyone else can beat it. That is, until "The Joystick Master" suddenly comes into town.

891. A popular computer game is released, and for two weeks straight, that's what everyone is talking about. Though, it is not for the graphics or even the gameplay. It's because of how people start to act afterward.

892. Your character is at a large gaming convention. They have spent weeks practicing their favorite game techniques, hoping to place in one of the tournaments. All of that practice seems to pay off. They've beaten every single match. Now, can they make it to the top?

893. With two degrees in literature, your character thought playing Scrabble would be both enjoyable and an easy way to get bragging rights from the rest of the family. They didn't expect to keep losing, especially to a child.

894. Your character has invented a new hopscotch game that has become all the rage at nightclubs everywhere. How exactly have they reinvented this usually innocent children's game into something a little more adult?

895. "Marco." "Polo." "Marco." "Polo" This isn't a children's game. Not just because these are adults playing, but the finder is getting closer and closer to their target. Your character hopes they aren't the one found first, because if so, it will be lights out for them.

Sports of All Sorts

Each year, billions of dollars are spent on sports, whether on fan merchandise or giving players million-dollar contracts. From globally televised matches to local leagues, we are obsessed with sports.

896. Your character has won tickets to the big football game. They are disappointed to find that their seats are in the nosebleed section. That is until they meet someone who invites them into the special-level club, where they can meet all their favorite players.

897. Your character is the star player on their high school basketball team. Every game, they show off their ability to make almost every shot. With just mere seconds left on the clock, they aim, jump, and shoot – only to miss just as the buzzer strikes.

898. Your character is rooting for their child at a little league baseball game along with all the other parents. When one of the players accidentally hits another with a fastball, a fight breaks out between the parents. Does your character try to stop it, join in, or instigate it further?

899. Your character is watching the ball fly back and forth between the players. They have never been that fond of tennis, thinking it a rather dull sport. All of that is about to change when something exciting happens. What is it?

900. Typically, hockey is known for being a too hands-on sport with the occasional bloodshed. However, this time, the players don't seem to have it in them to be rough and are overly polite to the point where they are barely playing. This, of course, incites the fans to violence. Your character included.

901. Your character competes in an intense surfing competition. However, the match is canceled when a surprise storm kicks up. Your character decides to stay, even when many of the professionals heed the warning. What could go wrong?

902. Your character is on a novice rowing team that hasn't even been on the water. While it doesn't come as a shock that the boat tips over a few times, it does come as a shock that one of them turns up missing.

903. A couple of teens are playing rugby on the street. It seems harmless enough, except they aren't paying attention to their surroundings. It isn't long before one of them kicks the ball through a shop window.

904. Freediving, a sport which involves going underwater for an extended period without any breathing equipment, is an exciting sport. Of course, it requires skill, but no one other sport allows one to swim alongside whales, run into a school of fish, or avoid hungry sharks all while holding one's breath. Suppose your character is doing this for the first time.

905. Your character narrows their eyes, steadies their arm, and lets the arrow fly. They are among the best archers globally, but this time they will miss on purpose, making the murder look like an accident.

906. Your character is a young teen that continually comes in last in track and field. One night something miraculous happens. They wake up, get read in 12 seconds, and run to school in 36 seconds. This time, they'll be coming in 1st place for sure.

907. While at the beach, your character gets asked to join in a friendly game of volleyball. Despite this being their first time playing, your character is surprisingly good. Really good! It just so happens, the people that have asked them to join in are professionals, and they ask your character to be their new teammate.

908. Roller derby is an underground but trendy sport. Your character is looking for something to do and decides to sign up. What they fail to tell their teammates is that they don't even know how to skate.

909. Your character is supposed to be one of the strongest people on Earth. Thus, it comes as no surprise that they enter and dominate an ax-throwing competition. They find the sport enjoyable and continue to do it. That is until they step up to the plate one and day and can't seem to lift even the smallest axes.

910. Your character has been a professional wrestler for many, many years. They've long since retired but have decided to join a local underground ring because of recent financial hardships. They are supposed to just be there for a photo op, but the organizers want them to step back into the ring.

911. Some will say cheerleading is not a sport, but your character disagrees with that sentiment entirely. Why? Are they a cheerleader? A coach? Or maybe they're just a huge fan?

912. Your character is in a group of synchronized swimmers that has been competing for a few years now. All of that work has paid off as they have finally made it to the Olympics. That's when tensions begin to rise, and the group threatens to break up.

913. While practicing for the upcoming figure skating season, your character lands a triple axel. Perhaps they should have vetted their practice location better because the ice breaks underneath their feet, and they crash into the icy water below.

914. During one misstep at a gymnastics competition, your character injures their ankle and needs to sit out for two weeks. What are they going to do to pass the time? To heighten the tension, consider what might happen if they cannot compete again.

915. Your character is a young child signed up for a softball league they do not want to participate in. No matter how much they press, their parents are relentless, hoping it will curb your character's wild behavior with some "structure." Your character immediately begins to plot ways to make them pay, on and off the softball field.

916. Your character is amongst a group of friends playing a friendly game of flag football. However, when lightning strikes and an unexpected thunderstorm rings out, some team members refuse to stop. Tensions run higher, and soon the game gets deadly.

917. While playing a game of polo, your character's horse suddenly stumbles to the ground. Your character has been in this support almost their entire life, and now, with an injury to the back, it seems they might never play again.

Wild Animals

Lions, tigers, and bears, *oh my!* Even though wild animals are all around us, both humans and animals alike tend to keep their distance from one another, from squirrels to alligators. In these prompts, all of that changes.

918. While on a hike, your near-sighted character sees what they think is a dog. It isn't until they are petting it and more "dogs" show, that they realize they are patting coyotes.

919. For a few days now, wild rabbits have been eating vegetables from your character's garden. They decide enough is enough and install a wooden fence. The rabbits still get in. They continue to get in despite wire, then stone fences. How is this happening?

920. Bleary-eyed, your character stirs inside their tent, rolling over and kissing their partner's cheek. Wait. This isn't right. Why is their partner suddenly bigger and *hairier*? This isn't their partner at all, but a wild bear!

921. Your character has signed up for the "meet and greet" portion of their wild sea life adventure. This means that they get to swim with dolphins. What the brochure failed to mention is that these particular dolphins are the ultimate pranksters. Soon your character finds themselves chasing after one of these marine hucksters, hoping to retrieve their swimming shorts.

922. It is a calm and serene day on the ocean. Your character presses in closer to their beloved as the two watch meandering whales together. Just when the two lean in for a kiss, one of them falls overboard.

923. While out on a safari, your character wanders too far from the rest of the group. The more they try to find their way back, the more lost they become. To make matters worse, they inadvertently get bitten by a venomous snake.

924. *Bump. Bump. Bump.* It seems that camel riding is not all it's cracked up to be, and your character already wants off. The camel seems to sense your character's annoyance and decides to run off at that exact moment.

925. While on a trip to the zoo, your character leads their child to the petting area. When your character and their family gets there, everyone's mouth drops down. You've never seen these animals at the petting zoo, or *any* zoo even.

926. On the subject of zoos, suppose your character is witness to a child falling into the enclosure of a dangerous animal. Will they jump in to save this child, or do they decide to be resourceful in some other way?

927. Your character is a part of an activist group set to release many circus animals in the dead of night. The group sneaks into one of the tents and is shocked at what they discover. The animals have already escaped! Your character hears a low growl behind them.

928. Suppose your character receives an invitation to go on a wild boar hunt. This is not entirely true. It turns out it is your character that will be hunted.

929. Somewhere down the gulf coast, your character is on a swamp tour. They are eager to see turtles, nutria, birds of all sorts, and *especially* alligators. The first few gators are pretty small, only 3 feet in length, but then comes out a giant monster! When it knocks the boat with its head, your character stumbles overboard, right into the murky water.

930. Your character is not a great swimmer, but somehow they have managed to swim out much further than they intended. Not only are they struggling to get back to shore, but they are also surrounded by a bunch of dorsal fins protruding from the water.

931. While at the beach, your character takes a bite of a delicious sandwich. At once, they begin to be surrounded by hungry seagulls. Reluctantly, your character feeds the birds, only to be surrounded by even more gulls. Then more and more. It's sheer madness!

932. Your character is a famous documentarian that has been primarily working with people, whether it's a film on corporate creed or true crime. Now they have been asked to film a nature documentary. This is totally out of their element, and they don't know the first thing about survival.

933. While on vacation in Asia, your character is attacked by a gang of wallet stealing monkeys. The assault is over in a few minutes, and the primates scamper off with the goods, including your character's cards and ID. How do they get back to the hotel?

934. Your character is a zoo veterinarian. Today's patient is a large tiger that is getting a rotten tooth removed. In the middle of the procedure, something growls. Your character's assistant has miscalculated the anesthesia dose. The tiger is waking up.

935. It is a beautiful place, the elephant sanctuary. Your character finds something serene about coming here and watching the roaming, gentle giants. One day something tragic happens. All the elephants have gone missing.

936. There are rumors of a super-intelligent squirrel on campus that will communicate with any student that gives them a treat. Your character, a freshman, assumes that this is a rumor merely told by the upperclassman. Then one day, a squirrel skitters by and begin to make strange gestures with its paw.

937. Your character, a mountain climber, falls into a ravine and breaks their leg. With no one knowing they are there and no way to call for help, your character thinks this may just be their last day on Earth. That is until a friendly mountain goat passes by, eager to help the injured adventurer.

938. Every night your character's trash cans are knocked over by a group of mischievous raccoons. Your character tries everything – from buying super tight lids to setting up booby traps. The raccoons get into the trash no matter what. This time your character waits outside all night to scare them off, but what they find isn't a group of raccoons at all.

Pets

They snuggle on our laps while watching movies with us, protect us from outsiders, and some must wear silly outfits. They are cats, dogs, rabbits, and anything else that is traditionally considered a pet.

939. Smoke billows throughout the air, along with the piercing shriek of the fire alarm. Your character has two small dogs under their arms and a bird sitting atop their head. They make their way outside, put the animals down, and go back inside the burning pet shop for more critters. Where the heck is the fire department?

940. Your character has just gotten a job at a dog kennel. With the title of "playtime assistant," they are excited to start work. While they are supposed to have puppies on their first day, the manager has somehow forgotten to communicate this with a co-worker. When the playroom door opens, out comes three large, unruly German Shepherds.

941. Your character is starting their day as a veterinarian's assistant. The first two patients are cats, both with general check-ups, the second is a dog with an ear infection, but the last is quite a doozy. Someone has brought in an unidentifiable creature. Even the vet is confused and alarmed.

942. Your character gets a new puppy for their birthday. They are thrilled. However, this is their very first pet, and training will fall squarely on their shoulders. How will they react to all the new responsibilities?

943. Your character has been dubbed a certified "cat lady." It isn't their fault they have too many cats. For, you see, it is the cats themselves that keep inviting new strays into the home.

944. "Krrrrrshhhkttttt.." It is the sound of cracking glass. Water begins to drip down onto the floor. Customers start looking around the restaurant, wondering what the noise is before someone worriedly points at the fish tank in the corner. The entire restaurant, both staff and guests, must work together to save over a dozen sea life before the tank breaks completely.

945. Your character's ferret is missing! They assume it is somewhere in the house and begin to search, room-by-room. They get to the final room, a small bathroom that hardly anyone uses, and there, illuminating the darkened space, is an open window.

946. "Get away from me! Get away from me!" The parrot squawks, over and over again. Since your character brought the bird home, it has refused to let anyone near them. What is making the parrot so agitated?

947. Your character is a judge at a very prestigious dog show. All of the canines are looking their very best, and your character has quite the work cut out for them. Little does your character know; one of the dog owners is cheating. What are they doing, and does your character catch wind?

948. On the reverse end of the spectrum, suppose your character is an owner of a cat show contestant. It is perfectly groomed, in good spirits, and is even being a little nicer than usual. That is until the judge gets eye level with your little fur baby. That's' when the claws come out.

949. Your character's pet is getting groomed for the first time. Encouraged by the groomer, your nervous character decides to do some shopping until their beloved pet is done. When they come back, their furry friend is a bald, shivering mess.

950. "Up!" The dog jumps on its hind legs and does a little dance at the command. "Rollover." The dog follows suit. Your character is quite impressed at the display. This isn't all the dog has learned. The dog can also be quite deadly, should the owner wish.

951. Your character wakes up to several babies inside their hamster's cage. Next to these little pink creatures are two proud looking parents. It seems your character has just become an accidental hamster breeder overnight.

952. No matter what your character does, their pet rabbit won't stop attacking anyone that chances for a visit. It's almost as if this rabbit has a thirst for blood - *human* blood.

953. After a relative dies unexpectedly, your character inherits their recently obtained puppy. This comes as quite an unwelcome surprise to the 12-year-old dog they already have. Despite the tragedy of losing their relative, your character soon finds solace in seeing this young pup and old dog become fast friends.

954. Your character is at their wit's end. Their friend started with one cat but now has nine and is already looking to adopt a few more kittens. This is incredibly unhealthy, and it is up to your character to find a way to curb their friend's feline addiction.

955. Using a similar scenario, suppose the friend isn't collecting cats, or even dogs, but snakes. Slithering, hissing snakes. Your character's friend has so many that a boa constrictor has someone gotten loose and is currently roaming around the neighborhood.

956. Oh no! While your character is attending a sleepover, their friend's tarantula goes missing. Your character is notorious for having arachnophobia, so their friends are scrambling to find the lost creature. It isn't long before your character feels something scuttle across their legs.

957. Your character is building their pet rabbit a wooden hutch, complete with a screen door. At least, that's the idea. Thus far, your character has gotten a splinter, buster their thumb with a hammer, and stubbed their toe several times. All while their pet bunny looks on helplessly.

958. Your character is a wealthy and influential individual who has been invited to a pet charity event. They arrive wearing a puppy dog onesie and are shocked that everyone else is wearing suits and dresses while walking or carrying their fur babies. It turns out; the instructions were to "bring your favorite pet," not "dress as your favorite pet." Your character probably should have listened to their assistant a little closer.

959. Your character's pet is a recent animal actor and has been featured in several films now. They've even gotten to waltz the red carpet. Over time, your character notices that the pet spends more time being a star and living a life of luxury than they do being another member of the family.

960. After their pet passes, your character is devastated. However, at the request of some friends, your character is also willing to get a new pet. Not as a replacement, but as a way to cope. Soon, they settle their eyes on a mangy little dog who ends up having a huge personality.

961. Your character is a world-renowned pet treat baker. Not only are their items beloved by millions, but they have even invented several new recipes. What the public doesn't know is that your character is allergic to most animals. Soon the secret will be out.

Food

Beyond needing it to live, we also use food in many different ways. As shown in previous sections, food can be a great unifier, bringing families and friends together. However, as you will see in this section, food can also be a great stress source.

962. It is the day of the great big cook-off! Your character has been preparing for months, perfecting their signature dish. Each contestant has precisely 1 hour to prepare then plate. During the competition, your character lets their nerves get the best of them. They burn all their food.

963. The vegetarian joint down the street is getting rave reviews. Everyone seems ecstatic about the new meatless burger. People assume the meat contains soy, chickpea, or some other type of plant. However, the truth is stranger.

964. After a few hours of hard work, your character has finished the big family feast. They decide to take a nap and awaken to the sound of firetrucks. Their house is on fire! How did this happen when they could have sworn the oven was off?

965. Your character decides to hold a bake sale to raise money even though they can't even prepare a boxed cake. This isn't going to stop them. They plan on putting a secret ingredient in the batter. What is it?

966. It's your character's first appearance on their very own cooking show. With the cameras rolling and their trademark grin firmly in place, they begin to demonstrate how to make one of their famous dishes. That's when the power goes out.

967. After the family reunion festivities died down, it is time for the big family dinner. Representatives from different generations are all seated at two large, long tables. It is going to be a night to remember, especially when the food fight breaks out.

968. Your character is anxiously awaiting the results from a seated food critic with pen in hand. Before the critic can finish writing down their final thoughts, they begin to sputter and gasp before falling over dead. Your character panics; it isn't long before they are blamed for the murder.

969. "Argh! Why can't I get this, right?" Your character is frustrated that they can't seem to nail down a recipe they found off a popular website. Their cupcakes explode for the fourth time. Little do they know that a hacker has changed the website's recipe, intending to cause chaos with frustrated bakers.

970. Your character is out shopping for groceries when something extraordinary happens. The food begins to fly off the shelves. Is it an Earthquake? Some type of alien attack? Did all of the food gain sentience? Just what exactly is going on?

971. Your character is at a neighborhood cookout. They are surprised to see one of the meanest neighbors of all participating in the festivities. That is until they secretly catch this neighbor, adding a vile ingredient in their dishes. What is it, and how does your character put a stop to it?

972. Breakfast is supposed to be the most important meal of the day. Your character takes this to heart by making a smoothie every morning with fresh ingredients from their garden. Since they have begun this routine, they are feeling worse, not better. This is because, unbeknownst to your character, someone has been spraying deadly poison on their beloved plants.

973. Your character is on a lunch date with someone they have been crushing after for quite some time. Everything seems to be going well, that is until your character's date has a big piece of spinach stuck in their teeth. Does your character tell them? Or resist the potential awkwardness?

974. Your character is the absolute worst in the cooking class they were excited to sign up for. Watching cooking shows on TV is one thing, but trying to cook is another. Does your character muster through or keep going, hoping to find the one dish they might excel at?

975. The mimosas are pouring, the eggs are poached, and the croissants are perfectly flaky. A group of friends has been having Sunday brunch together for the past ten years. This brunch is about to get a little more morose. One of the friends announces that they only have a few months to live.

976. Due to a global pandemic, your character must have all their food delivered. One day, they are ordering their usual lunch when they notice a package with a note on it. A love note! This starts a back and forth romance between your character and the food delivery person.

977. Your character has been foraging food for the past few months, ever since they decided to live off the grid and have a more quiet, peaceful existence. Things have been going well, and they find life more serene, but they miss their home, especially when they think of all the junk foods they used to eat. One day, they discover a sealed package containing their favorite fast food. The next day, it's another fast food place. Is someone out there reading their mind?

978. For the past several weeks, your character has woken up every night with a horrific case of acid reflux. At first, they could quickly point to the greasy pizzas and burgers they had, but now even a salad will make them wake up gasping for air. What is wrong with them? Write a medical tale in which your character is diagnosed and treated. Remember to do your research or consult a professional.

979. Down on their luck, your character has taken to scouring the dumpsters looking for food. It is a horrifying reality for many, and your character now has an insider's perspective. Soon good fortune will find them because they find more than just food to sustain themselves. They also see something precious, as well. What is this valuable item that isn't money?

980. On the opposite end of the spectrum, your character is a billionaire who has more money than they could ever use in one lifetime. After a run-in with the law, your character must work at a food bank, seeing how the other half lives for the first time. Will this help them change their ways, or is your character too selfish to care?

981. Your character can't stop eating! They eat a giant burger, then three large fries, then another two burgers, 12 chicken nuggets, a milkshake, and are still hungry during lunch. This isn't a case of someone having a medical issue, but suppose it is a strange case of revenge from a magical fairy. How did they upset the creature, and why has the fairy decided to punish them this way?

Finances

There is a reason why money is supposed to be the root of all evil. It corrupts, it is hard to get, and it can often mean life or death. Whether your character has too little or too much, these prompts deals with the monetary needs we all have.

982. Your character can't believe their eyes. After almost two decades of playing, they have finally won the lottery! They are officially a multimillionaire. Not even two minutes into planning what they'll do with the winnings, their phone begins to ring. It doesn't stop.

983. When your character pays for their expensive meal, including all their friends' plates, the waiter comes back and sheepishly indicates that the card was declined. This happens with *all* of their credit cards. Your character has lost access to the joint accounts they share, but why? More importantly, how is their partner able to get away with this?

984. Your character has just been robbed. The crook is now running away with your character's purse or wallet. Karma must be out in full force since your character stole the item from someone else.

985. "Ready? Let's go!" Your character pulls down the mask and bursts through the doors of the bank. "Everybody down!" With their adrenaline pumping, your character forces everybody to the ground while their comrades work on the safe. With sirens in the distance, there's no telling if they'll make it out alive.

986. These numbers can't be right. Your character scrolls down the financial statement on their computer. Everything seemed normal a week ago. But, these numbers don't lie. It appears Your character's accountant has been sabotaging the figures for their own personal gain.

987. Your character finds a lost wallet on the side of the road while walking. Instinctively, they pick it up and see a wad of cash sticking out. Does your character return the wallet sans money, keep everything, or return it in the original condition?

988. Your character moves to a small town where everyone knows everyone. After introducing themselves at the local grocer, they are surprised to learn that they share the last name with the wealthiest family. Do they use this link to Old Money to their advantage? If so, how?

989. On the opposite end of the spectrum, suppose your character is New Money, meaning that they have only recently become wealthy. How much has their life changed now that they can now buy whatever they want? Do people in their small town treat them differently?

990. Under the weight of student loans, your character is suffering. They haven't even touched the principle on their 140k balance. Then they get an offer they can't refuse. Commit a crime and get the entirety of their loan paid off.

991. Your character is working three jobs just to make ends meet. This doesn't seem to be enough because every time they get ahead, something else happens. To make matters worse, they get harassed at one of these jobs. Spin a tale of revenge that also sees this character become financially stable in the end.

992. Your character is an avid urban explorer, finding and investigating abandoned and lost places. They discover an old house that has remained untouched for centuries. Inside they find a room filled to the brim with gold bars.

993. Your character has been wealthy their entire life. Now that they are reaching the end of it, they find being the richest person on Earth isn't all that it is cracked up to be. They decide to give all of their money away. How do they go about it?

994. "3 million dollars," the masked figure barks into the phone before hanging up. The culprit turns back to your character and grins. "If they don't pay, you die." Your character is a ransom to a wealthy family. What the abductor doesn't know is they have the wrong person.

995. After a busy day at work, your character comes home to find the babysitter asleep and their toddler in the middle of the room. Balled up in their tiny little fists are wads of cash, which do not belong to the babysitter or your character.

996. Your character is a known purse snatcher who has never been caught. This time is no different, but instead of finding the usual cash and credit cards, the purse only contains coins and lifesaving medication. Does your character decide to return it?

997. Your character comes to work and discovers they have a new manager. They are immediately given new job responsibilities, and by the end of the day, they are exhausted. By the end of the week, your character is ready to burst into tears. How do they combat the unfairness of this new manager's treatment?

998. In a heavily secured vault, your character is opening their security box with shaky hands. Inside is a secret. What is it, and why are they so desperate to keep it?

999. Your character is not a criminal mastermind, but they have been stealing millions from the company they work for. How have they accomplished this feat? By stealing half a cent per transaction for the last three years.

1000. Your character wakes up to good news—sort of. A relative has passed and left them a considerable inheritance. Sadly, the relative is deceased, but with this money, your character's life is about to change forever.

1001. One week ago, your character lived in a penthouse in one of the most populated cities in the world. Now, they are homeless with the last 2 dollars in their pocket. What happened?

ABOUT THE AUTHOR

Christina Escamilla is the bestselling author of psychological horror with a side of nonfiction, both in analysis and literary theory and the craft of writing. Aside from working on her next book, she is currently working on multiple writing courses for the spring and summer of 2021.

She is also the founder and co-owner of the marketing education hub, Glacial Edge. The organization offers marketing courses, resources, and articles to help small business owners.

When she is not working or writing, Escamilla is an avid traveler, coffeeshop haunter, and antique and oddity enthusiast. She currently spreads her time between Pensacola, Florida, and Houston, Texas, with her partner Tyler, and their two furbabies, Tapioca the dog and Angel the cat.

Find her on the web at stinaesc.com

Facebook, Twitter, Instagram: stinaesc

Printed in Great Britain
by Amazon

38929800R00138